Training Sales Associates For Success

Michael L. Jewell, CRB, CRS

A publication of the
Real Estate Brokerage Council™ of the
REALTORS NATIONAL MARKETING INSTITUTE®,
an affiliate of the
NATIONAL ASSOCIATION OF REALTORS®.

Real Estate Brokerage Council™
430 N. Michigan Ave.
Chicago, IL 60611-4092

International Standard Book Number: 0-913652-76-8
Library of Congress Catalog Card Number: 90-21103
Real Estate Brokerage Council™ Catalog Number: 145

Printed in the United States of America
First Printing, 1991, 3,000 copies

Table of Contents

Introduction   v
1. Aspects of Training   1
   Benefits to the Company
   Benefits to the Sales Associates
   Misconceptions about Training
   Adults as Learners
2. Planning for Training   11
   Training and Your Strategic Plan
   Developing a Training Program
3. Identifying Training Needs   17
   Company/Office Needs
   Sales Associate Needs
4. Establishing Training Objectives   25
   General and Specific Objectives
5. Budgeting Considerations   29
   Approaches to Budgeting
   Cost Areas
6. Selecting and Organizing Content   33
7. Selecting Equipment and Materials   37
8. Determining Trainers and Training Methods   43
   Trainer Characteristics
   Training Environment
   Scheduling
   Presentation Methods
   Five Stages of Training
   Training Hints
9. Evaluating Results and Reinforcing Training   59

10. Ongoing Training   61

Instructor's Outline
Possible Topics for Continuous Training
Summary

Appendix A: Sample Training Program   73
Appendix B: Forms   93
Index   99

Introduction

Training Sales Associates for Success, the complementary text to Certified Real Estate Brokerage Manager (CRB®) Course 304, is for anyone responsible for training sales associates. This book introduces sales managers and broker/owners to effective sales training methods that provide a solid foundation for developing productive salespeople in most selling situations. It also describes the training process in detail while remaining uncomplicated and reader friendly.

Using the practical outline provided, you will be able to develop a training program that can be adapted to the needs of associates who are new to the business or to those who simply need a refresher in a specific area of real estate sales. Your efforts to train these individuals will pay financial rewards to you, to them, and to the company, and you will experience the satisfaction of knowing you have helped your salespeople increase their selling abilities and earning power.

1

Aspects of Training

To define training, one must recognize the difference between training and education. Education, in the traditional sense, means to impart knowledge. Education is helping people know and understand facts, concepts and theories. Education focuses on the "thinking" process. As people become "educated," they build up a storehouse of information that can be used throughout life.

Training, on the other hand, is showing people how to use and apply their knowledge to accomplish something, to develop a skill. Training focuses on the "doing" process. From a business standpoint, training is putting knowledge to consistent and profitable use. Profitability can be seen in terms of dollars, personal growth, new skills learned, etc. As individuals being trained are rewarded, so is the organization. This is the key reason why training is so important. When conducted correctly and consistently, and with ongoing reinforcement and performance evaluation, training pays great dividends to both the individual and the organization.

A training *program* is a planned, consistent and timely approach to showing new and experienced sales associates how to achieve their own and their company's objectives.

Training would be easy if it were as simple as the above definition. In reality, training combines education and skill development, plus much more. When you train people, you in effect make them change their behavior. "Behavior" as used here means how, when and where associates conduct their sales activities. If you can persuade them to use new, more productive behavior patterns consistently for a period of time, their behavior will become habitual. As they become more comfortable, they will develop a positive attitude about what they are doing. This attitude will reinforce the behavior and enhance the development of good selling habits. Successful selling habits lead to productivity, which leads to financial success for the salespeople and the company.

Behavior development or change is accomplished through two different management functions: sales training and sales management. The trainer initiates the process of developing or changing behavior. Because training groups typically are large and therefore time spent with individual participants usually is short, the trainer only has a limited opportunity to make a lasting impression on each individual's behavior. By demonstrating the proper behavior and making the participants practice it several times, the trainer and the group get off to a great start in developing lasting habits.

The full challenge of changing behavior and developing good, productive selling habits falls on the sales manager, however. Only in the rare instance when a sales associate is a self-starter and a self-motivator will little management reinforcement or assistance be necessary. In all other cases, the manager must work almost daily with associates to foster the transition from their beginning behavior upon entering the business to their full development as successful sales associates.

As already implied, training focuses on three areas: knowledge, skill and attitude. While most training programs encompass all three, specific training sessions may concentrate on one. For example, if a new type of financing becomes available in your marketplace and your sales associates already know how to qualify buyers, most of your training effort should be aimed at helping them learn how the new financing works. Or if your associates understand the techniques of qualifying yet still are not doing a good job of dealing with potential buyers, you must further develop their ability to use and communicate their knowledge. If they have the knowledge and skill and are not using it, chances are they need to be injected with a little enthusiasm; you must improve their attitude about dealing with buyers. Specific training sessions can satisfy these needs. However, training sessions don't have to be limited to concentrating on just one of the three areas of training. Any two or all three of the training areas may need to be dealt with. Determining what areas to cover will be discussed in Chapter 3, "Identifying Training Needs."

So how does all this take place in the training environment? First, you must be certain to impart the basic knowledge that the sales associates need to learn the skill. Note the word "basic." If, for example, you want salespeople to develop the ability to call on For Sale By Owners (FSBOs), you should not complicate the process by trying to teach them the ins and outs of purchase agreements, financing and the closing process all at the same time. Simply provide the information on how to call on an FSBO, then help them develop the ability to put that information to use. You can do this by creating a role-playing situation in the office and letting them practice. As you will see later, role playing involves more than just acting. It involves "playing a part" while being coached, evaluated and receiving feedback from everyone involved. After the salespeople have learned to apply their new knowledge in this safe environment, send them out into the real world—preferably accompanied the first few times by someone who is experienced. Again, this first venture into the marketplace needs to be evaluated and the associates need to receive plenty of feedback.

You have given the sales associates the basic knowledge necessary for developing the skill of calling on FSBOs and have sent them out into the marketplace. No doubt they will meet with some rejection. But if the first goal you set for them simply is to make contact and to establish some rapport, they probably will meet with some success as well. You have cleared the first hurdle of getting your associates out to do something. This is what training is all about: Teaching someone how to apply knowledge in segments that build toward learning a complete skill in a specific area such as listing, selling, communicating, etc. As the sales associates' experience grows, so will their confidence and their attitude in whatever they are attempting to accomplish.

Let's step back and see what we have covered. Knowledge and skill development change or modify behavior, which when repeated often result in newly formed habits that lead to success. To conclude this discussion, we must review the four learning stages of the training process: unconscious incompetency, conscious incompetency, conscious competency and unconscious competency.

Let's use learning to ski as our example. Even though people may have watched others ski, they really don't know how much they don't *know*. They are *unconscious incompetents*. Now put some boots and skis on them and put poles in their hands. A few falls will serve to teach them that there's a lot they don't know. They have become *conscious incompetents*. They *know* what they don't know.

After taking lessons and practicing, the new skiers can get on and off the chair lifts and can make reasonably smooth runs. They are now *conscious competents*. They know what to do and they can do it, yet they have to constantly think hard about what they are doing to make it happen.

With consistent, frequent practice, they move to the highest level, the *unconscious competent*. They now look and act like the skiers they used to watch. They make runs without really having to think about what they are doing. By acquiring knowledge and applying it to develop a skill, they exhibit a new behavior. And through ongoing practice, they develop a good attitude about their ability. Another way of looking at it is this: They have developed a good *habit*.

But beware. In real estate, just as in skiing, people do not always remain on the unconscious-competent level. By not practicing, they can drift back to the level of conscious competent, or worse (and rarer), conscious incompetent. As a sales manager with training responsibilities, you must watch for this backwards drifting and take appropriate action, such as one-on-one counseling, coaching, or additional training.

As an old proverb says:

"You can give a man a fish [educate, impart knowledge]
and he can eat for a day.
You can teach him to fish [train, develop skill]
and he can eat for a lifetime."

Benefits to the Company

A number of benefits can result from establishing and conducting training programs within a company or its individual offices. To gain these benefits, training must become an integral part of the organization's weekly activities.

Increase Profits

All of the following benefits help achieve higher profit levels. By training new and experienced salespeople, evaluating their sales performance, and providing them with feedback, a company virtually can assure itself of improving its bottom line. The following example illustrates this point.

For one month, CRB Realty's classified advertising cost $3,500 and resulted in 100 calls. The cost per inquiry was $35 ($3,500 ÷ 100).

- From these 100 inquiries, the company's salespeople were able to obtain 20 buyer-qualification appointments. Thus, it took five ad responses to get one appointment—a conversion factor of 20 percent.
- Ten offers were generated from the 20 appointments. Thus, two appointments were needed for each offer, a conversion factor of 50 percent.
- Six sales resulted from the 10 offers, meaning it took 1.7 offers to make one sale. This equals a 60 percent success factor.
- Finally, 4.8 closings were accomplished from the six sales. Thus, 1.25 sales were needed for each closing—an 80 percent success factor.

If this figure is applied to the classified advertising cost, the advertising cost per closed sale can be determined:

- $35 x 5 (number of inquiries to get one appointment) = $175 per appointment.
- $175 × 2 (number of appointments needed for each offer) = $350 per offer.
- $350 × 1.7 (number of offers needed per sale) = $595 per sale.
- $595 × 1.25 (number of sales for one closing) = $744 per closing.

Therefore, the advertising cost per closed sale is $744.

You could have divided the advertising cost by the 4.8 closed sales. This would have shown a $729 advertising cost per sale (difference is due to rounding). Determining cost this way would not, however, provide you with the opportunity to see the benefits from improving one or more of the sales involved with achieving closed sales.

If CRB Realty trained its salespeople to become more effective in converting ad calls to appointments and everything else remained constant, the company could achieve a substantial reduction in advertising cost allocation per sale because it would make more sales from the same number of advertising dollars spent. If the conversion of inquiries to appointments increased from 20 to 30 per 100, the company would realize quite an impact on the cost per closed sale.

- 100 inquiries results in 30 appointments (3.33 calls per appointment).
- $35 × 3.33 = $116.55 per appointment.
- $116.55 × 2 = $233.10 per offer (30 appointments x 50% = 15 offers).
- $233.10 × 1.7 = $396.27 per sale (15 offers × 60% = 9 sales).
- $396.27 × 1.25 = $495.34 per closed sale (9 sales × 80% = 7.2 closed sales).

The results would be a potential profit increase of $248.41 per sale ($743.75 – 495.34) if the effectiveness of the salespeople in handling ad inquiries increased from 20 to 30 appointments per 100 calls. By improving just one of the steps to achieving closed sales, the number of sales increases from 4.8 to 7.2.

Training, therefore, can have quite an impact on profits. In the previous example the advertising costs remained the same, while the net profits increased simply by training the salespeople to generate more closed sales from the same number of calls. Training can exert a positive impact on your bottom line in other ways as well: more listings, more listings that are priced to sell, more effective marketing of listings, improved buyer qualifications, a lower ratio of showings to sales, and a smaller fall-through (sale/fail) rate.

Improve the Company Image

The more thoroughly trained your sales associates are, the better prepared they will be to represent your company in the marketplace. This creates a positive image of your company for the public.

Your sales associates play a key part in your company's overall marketing program. Basically, in the service industry marketing can be defined as all the activities involved in conceiving, developing and delivering services that are intended to satisfy customer needs and wants as a means of achieving company goals. Ironically, this definition represents the culmination of an evolutionary process that initially had little to do with customer satisfaction.

In the past, companies focused on producing products without much regard for the public's needs or wants. In doing so, they often failed to recognize what business they really were in. Classic examples include the railroad companies that thought they were in the railroad business instead of in the transportation business and the movie companies that produced movies without fully realizing that they were in the entertainment business. Had these companies clearly understood the nature of the businesses they were in, other companies in industries such as trucking, aviation, shipping, television and radio might have different owners today.

Coupled with this focus on product was a focus on selling. The belief was that whatever the product or service, they could sell it. This resulted in a high failure rate for products and services, little concern for quality, alienation of customers, image problems for the industry producing and selling the particular product or service and, because customers' needs and wants were not being fully satisfied, increased competition. In an effort to improve the situation and become more successful, some companies began to ask, "What is it that the customer really needs and wants?" This question paved the way to customer orientation.

Customer orientation is an effort to match the customers' needs and wants with what a company has available or can produce. This approach has redefined the term "marketing" and has divided the marketing program concept into four basic parts: product/service mix, price, place/delivery systems, and promotion. These four parts form what is referred to as the marketing mix. Your salespeople are the key element of the marketing mix. For this reason, training must be designed to maximize the positive impact a salesperson can have in each of these four areas as well as on the overall integrated marketing program.

A company's personality is formed in large part by the *products and services* it handles. If your sales associates are not adequately trained, they may not be able to deal with the types of products and services that you want to be representative of your company.

They also may be unprepared to deliver and explain the menu of products and services that you have developed. Thus, your salespeople can exert a positive or a negative effect on your product/service mix and on the resulting image of your company.

Similarly, your *pricing* policies will be carried out mainly by your salespeople. Incorrectly priced property may not sell, thereby negatively affecting your company's image. In addition, if your salespeople are not properly trained to present themselves and the company, they may have difficulty convincing sellers that the marketing fee is appropriate.

With *place/delivery systems*, a number of methods are available for delivering products and services to the market. Even so, your sales force still is the primary method.

Finally, *promotion* is how your company communicates with the marketplace. Advertising, public relations and sales promotion are important, yet they will be inadequate if the fourth element, your salespeople, falls short in presenting what you are trying to accomplish through these other methods of marketing communications. Much of your advertising expenditure will be wasted if your associates do not consistently project the image that you are trying to get the public to accept.

Your associates' ability to work with your marketing mix combined with their ability to effectively communicate can improve and enhance your company image, your marketing results and your profits.

Recruit More Associates

Because of the rapid changes occurring within the real estate industry, people entering the business want to know how a company will assist them to become financially successful. A complete training program often is the answer they are looking for from a company. Not offering a training program can cause a company to appear less desirable to new and experienced salespeople alike, especially if the competition offers training.

Terminate Inadequate Associates

Sales associates with little potential for success should be eliminated. While this unpleasant but necessary task is usually handled by the sales manager, it can be done by the trainer if he or she has the authority to make termination decisions. Or, if the trainer doesn't have that authority, he or she should be encouraged to make recommendations to the management.

If a salesperson, new or experienced, enters your training program and is unwilling or unable to complete assignments, exercises, etc., you can fairly accurately assume that the individual will not be successful at sales. This determination must be made on an individual basis, and guidelines should be established to help with the decision process. After all, if someone will not or cannot complete the basics, he or she probably will have little chance of being successful in listing and selling.

Improve Communications and Work Habits

The better your salespeople understand what they are expected to do, how they are to do it, and the results they should expect, the better they will be able to communicate with you. They also will have a much higher potential for developing good work habits. In addition to the possibility of increased production, you will not have to closely supervise these individuals. This is a tremendous benefit in a business with constant time pressures.

Control Turnover

If the first five benefits are achieved, associates will be less likely to leave your company. They will earn more quickly than their counterparts in the business and they will feel good about the company. This can go a long way toward helping you control turnover, especially turnover of associates you do not want to lose.

Benefits to the Sales Associates

Sales associates also can derive a number of benefits from a well-developed and well-conducted training program. The benefits are as follows:

• **The Ability to Achieve Higher Earnings.** If people are given the knowledge necessary to be successful sales associates and are trained to develop the skills to use this knowledge, they will have a much higher potential for success. With frequent evaluation on how they are doing, they will develop effective work habits and a sense of security. If their earnings fall within their desired range, they can be less concerned about the future. In turn, the associates can focus on the activities necessary for increasing earnings.

• **Increased Self-Confidence.** The more time people have to learn and practice, the better they feel about what they are trying to accomplish. To just be "turned loose" to learn by trial and error can be very defeating. A quality training program allows for practice in a "safe" environment, and even though the associates still may experience failures in the field, those failures will occur less frequently. As a result, the associates feel good about what they are doing and will want to continue.

• **Recognition of Accomplishments.** Recognition is critically important to most people. While success will result only from their efforts, training will help them get off to a good start and will keep them moving forward in a positive direction. This will lead to worthwhile accomplishments and form the basis for you and others to recognize their achievements.

Misconceptions About Training

Almost everyone who has entered real estate sales has heard some of the following misconceptions about selling, all of which relate to the need or lack of need for training.

• **"Experience is the Best Teacher."** There is no question that experience is a teacher. The problem with this statement is the use of the word "best." Many times people learn the wrong information and/or skills from experience, and it takes more time and effort to "unlearn" what doesn't work so they can relearn what does work. Training combined with supervised experience provides the best of both worlds.

• **"Practice Makes Perfect."** Without a doubt, people must practice to become good at an activity. Yet practicing the wrong method does no good at all. Training exposes people to the correct methods that they can practice to become effective and successful.

• **"Only Hard Work Leads to Success."** Sure, you must work hard to enjoy financial success in sales. Still, it is a good idea to work smart as well as hard. Training provides the "smart" approach.

• **"Don't Memorize Your Presentation."** A memorized presentation usually comes across as "canned." Unfortunately, many hear this statement and do not memorize anything. As a result, they may get lost during a presentation or forget to include key points. This often inhibits their ability to successfully conclude the presentation, and a sale or listing can be lost.

Some memorization is critical. Without it, no one would be able to move through the four stages of learning to reach the unconscious-competent level. The best approach is to memorize key elements of the presentation to a buyer or seller, while remaining flexible at the same time. This enables the associate to respond comfortably and candidly to comments and questions.

• **"We Will Train You."** This probably is the biggest misconception about real estate sales training. Many companies offer training programs, yet few do a good job of fulfilling the offer. People are looking for good training and usually are quick to note an inadequate program. To obtain and maintain a competitive edge, you must offer the best training in your marketplace.

Keeping these misconceptions in mind will help you to design, implement and evaluate your training program. As a result, you and your associates should realize increased financial rewards.

Adults as Learners

Much research has been conducted and a great deal of time and money have been spent studying adults as learners. From this vast amount of research, valuable information has been gained.

For example, adults typically do not follow a plan and consequently don't make good learners. Of course, children do not follow a plan either, but they seem to have the ability to absorb more information and are more flexible. Adults tend to fear peer pressure; they are more concerned about failing. Children experience similar fears, but the fears are not as highly developed as those of adults. Adults, unlike children, enter a learning environment with a critical attitude—a "show me" attitude. Instructors, therefore, must win them over quickly so that learning can take place.

There are other considerations when teaching, or training, adults. Among them is the fact that adults can be highly resistant to change. The older they get, the greater that resistance seems to be. Adults also seem to have relatively bad learning habits. While they might have been good students at one time, many tend to forget their good learning habits as time goes on. Finally, adults become bored more easily, leading to irritation and the loss of any desire to learn. This boredom usually results from covering information that they already may have learned. Their attention span can be very short. As a result, adult training must be a mixture of facts, activities and humor to keep them involved and interested.

The key is to think about what you would expect as a participant walking into a training session. What outcome would you want? Granted, this is not a completely fair question. New associates, for example, may have only a vague notion of what they want. They probably will be openminded at first. Still, you will have only a few minutes to create a good first impression that makes them look forward to hearing and doing more.

One last comment about adult learners. Like children, they enjoy being entertained. This can take the form of humorous stories, examples of real-life experiences, etc. Just be sure that the entertainment does not hinder your efforts to develop your associates' knowledge, skills and positive attitudes; i.e., the beginning of successful selling habits. Otherwise, you may end up with a lot of happy but nonproducing sales associates.

2

Planning
for Training

To achieve full potential from your training activities, you should incorporate training as part of your company or office plan. Doing this will help you accomplish your training objectives because you will be able to a) determine how to use training most effectively in your company, and b) better measure the effectiveness of your training.

Training and Your Strategic Plan

By now just about everyone has heard of or been exposed to strategic planning. Keep in mind that any type of planning basically asks where you have been and are now (situation analysis), who you are (mission statement), where you want to go (objectives), how you will get there (strategies and tactics), how you will know when you have arrived (measurement), and what the cost will be (budget). One form of strategic planning is referred to as the SMOST approach.

The *situation analysis* is your evaluation of the marketplace and your company to determine past and present factors. The results of this detailed analysis will help you develop the rest of your plan.

The *mission statement* describes your company, its reason for existence, and its overall philosophy. (While some feel that the mission statement should be the first step, we'll leave it as step two.)

Objectives are statements of what you want to accomplish. Having too many objectives for your company or office may prove confusing and could result in less being accomplished instead of more.

Strategies are fairly broad statements about accomplishing your objectives. They should include such considerations as how, when, who and what. Finally, *tactics* are specific, short-lived actions that will help you accomplish your strategies.*

Rather than go into a detailed example of a situation analysis, assume that it is your marketplace and you are knowledgeable about past and present factors. Also assume that you have a mission statement that, in effect, says you will earn a profit by serving your market in a professional and ethical manner and by providing a good working environment for your people. For objectives you might list the following:

Objective 1:
Increase market share in present markets by _____ percent.

Objective 2:
Increase pretax profits to _____.

Objective 3:
Increase closed-transaction productivity by _____ percent.

Training can have a definite impact on these three objectives. Increasing closed-transaction productivity is a good example of how training plays an integral part in your plan.

For strategies and tactics you might list the following:

Strategy 1:
By _____ 19_____, develop a training program to assist experienced sales associates in increasing their production by _____ percent.

Tactics:
1. Determine current level of productivity per associate by _____ 19_____ .

2. By _____ 19_____ , develop specific weekly training sessions to increase/improve experienced sales associates' knowledge, sales skills and attitude toward accomplishing their goals and the company's objectives.

3. By _____ 19_____ , implement weekly training sessions developed in Tactic 2 to keep experienced associates current and productive and to reinforce previous training.

4. By _____ 19_____ , implement an evaluation system to measure the success of the training program in regard to the associates' monthly, quarterly and yearly production goals.

---

*For a detailed examination of the SMOST approach, refer to *Strategic Planning for the Real Estate Manager* by Ken Reyhons, CRB, CRS, published by the Real Estate Brokerage Council™ of the REALTORS NATIONAL MARKETING INSTITUTE®, an affiliate of the NATIONAL ASSOCIATION OF REALTORS®.

Strategy 2:
By _____ 19_____ , review and revise the training program for new salespeople based on their obtaining _____ listings and _____ sales within their first _____ days on the job.

Tactics:
1. Evaluate past performance of new salespeople by _____ 19_____ .

2. Establish minimum time periods for obtaining listings and making sales by _____ 19_____ .

3. By _____ 19_____ , review current program for training new associates to determine if it maximizes their potential for attaining the levels of production set forth in this strategy within the time frames set forth in this strategy.

4. Revise training as necessary by _____ 19_____ .

5. Test with a group of new salespeople by _____ 19_____ .

6. Make additional revisions if necessary and complete by _____ _____ 19_____ .

7. By _____ 19_____ , develop and implement a system for monitoring the effectiveness of the training program and the success of new salespeople.

When developing your strategies and tactics, you should also specify who will be responsible for accomplishing them. For example:

Strategy 1:
By _____ 19_____ , develop a training program to assist experienced sales associates in increasing their productivity by _____ percent. (To be accomplished by ___*name*___ .)

You might be wondering, "Is this amount of detail necessary?" Maybe not, yet you must follow some type of plan if you want to maximize the potential for productivity of your salespeople. Don't be overly concerned with the beauty of your finished plan. The process is as important as the finished product. If you want to accomplish something, you need a direction and an outline of how to do it. You need a plan. To help you create your plan, you must conduct a needs analysis, which is the first of seven steps in developing a training program.

Developing a Training Program

Seven steps are involved in developing a training program. While arguments could be made to increase or decrease the number of steps, the following seven do a good job of outlining the basic elements in the development process. Each will be covered in more detail in following chapters.

• **Step 1: Identifying Training Needs.** The first question to ask yourself is this: "Does your company need a training program?" While the obvious answer most likely will be "yes," training is not the solution to every problem.

Needs analysis should determine your office or company training needs. Basically, these needs will be the difference between existing conditions, activities, production, etc., and what you feel they should be or want them to be.

You also must determine the needs of your sales associates—both new and experienced—as related to their performance under current market conditions.

• **Step 2: Establishing Learning Objectives.** Learning objectives ask the question, "What should the participant know and be able to do as a result of the training?" Then they answer that question. While training focuses on the "doing" process, some knowledge development probably will be necessary for the participants to be able to fully perform the skill that is being learned.

• **Step 3: Budget Considerations.** This could be the first step depending on your organization. Many companies allocate a specific amount for training at the beginning of the year. It becomes the trainer's challenge to use this limited resource to its best advantage.

If this is not the first step in your company, a budget can be established at this point or after any of the next three steps.

• **Step 4: Selecting and Organizing Content.** Based on your learning objectives, you must determine what knowledge you must impart and what skills you must develop in your sales associates to enable them to successfully achieve their objectives and company objectives.

• **Step 5: Selecting Equipment and Materials.** In this step, your goal is to choose and/or develop items that will capture and maintain the attention of your training participants and enhance the training process by making it more interesting and enjoyable.

• **Step 6: Determining Instructors and Instructional Materials.** This step includes a multitude of factors, such as instructor characteristics, scheduling, methods of presenting the material, and the training environment. This is where everything comes together and training is conducted.

• **Step 7: Evaluating Results and Reinforcing Training.** It often has been said that, "If it's worth doing, it's worth measuring the results." This is especially true of training, for the results must appear both in the training environment and in the field. Herein lies a difference. Regardless of who conducts the training program, they must help the participants fulfill the desired objectives through knowledge, skill and attitude development. Behavior change only begins with training. Because behavior change comes from repetition, reinforcing training in the field is as important as, if not more important than, the actual training experience. This reinforcement is the responsibility of the sales manager.

These seven steps may appear to be too numerous and too involved, but do not be dissuaded from following them. Depending on the type and complexity of your needs, the seven steps can be quite easy to use, even if some of them only serve as a means for reviewing your program's content, equipment, material and instructors, or as a source of available resources.

3

Identifying Training Needs

Does your company really need a training program? The obvious answer to this question is "yes," especially if you desire increased productivity and profits. As discussed previously, training can pay big rewards. Yet many real estate companies do not provide an adequate training program, and some offer none at all.

Company/Office Needs

Your answers to the following questions should help you more fully view your office's or company's potential needs for training and the specific areas where training could produce the greatest returns.

	Yes	No	Priority

1. Does the success of your company/office depend on the knowledge, skills and attitudes of your sales associates?
2. Does the mission statement of your company/office refer to the behavior of your sales associates with each other, other brokers and the general public?
3. Do the objectives, strategies and tactics of your company/

	Yes	No	Priority

office require sales associates to know and carry out specific activities?

4. Do you plan to expand the market area of your company/office?

5. Are you trying to increase the market share of your company/office in existing markets?

6. Are you planning to enter any new market areas in the near future?

7. Are you starting to sell different types of properties that are new to your company/office, such as condominiums, recreational property, vacant land?

8. Are you considering new services to offer the public, such as mortgages, insurance, warranty programs, relocation?

9. Are you attempting to conduct business with new groups of people (new target markets)?

10. Have you encountered changes in your marketplace, such as new approaches to financing, a seller's market becoming a buyer's market, new competition?

11. Do you have any special needs, such as obtaining more listings or sales, or dealing with a problem development?

12. Are you in the process of recruiting and affiliating with new associates?

13. Are your sales associates, individually and as a group, as productive as you want them to be?

14. Do your primary competitors offer training programs?

15. Do you want to increase your bottom-line profits?

Look back over your "yes" answers. Rank each of them in order of priority, giving your most pressing need a ranking of one, your second most pressing a two, and so on. Now you have a list indicating potential areas for general and specialized training. Use this list to construct specific objectives, to design program content and delivery, and to plan activities to build sales skills in your associates.

Keep in mind that changes in the marketplace, financing innovations, increased competition and a variety of other variables may force you to reconsider your training needs and revise your program. To keep your training program as vibrant and as effective as possible, you should review your company's/office's needs at least quarterly and make any necessary changes or additions.

Answering the preceding questions will provide you with areas of training for your company/office. You also must determine which sales associates need training and what type of training will best fill their needs: knowledge, skill, attitude, or a combination of all three.

Sales Associate Needs

There are four groups of people in any real estate company/office who require different types and degrees of training. The first group, and the one that demands the most time, is new sales associates. While new associates may have taken some courses to obtain their real estate licenses, chances are they do not know how to put this information to use. And teachers of licensing courses usually do not spend a lot of time on selling techniques or other areas of practical application.

In most cases, new sales associates have little if any selling experience and thus need a great deal of skill development. They also need constant reinforcement about their decision to enter the real estate business so they will continue to feel good about it. This group requires a considerable investment of your time, not only initially, but on an ongoing basis to be certain that they put what they've learned into practice. These associates require group and one-on-one training.

The second group consists of associates who have performed fairly well in the business and currently are in a slump. These associates need a lot of personal attention and counseling, help in rethinking goals and activities, and probably a return to the basics. This could involve sharpening their skills, reviewing the basic aspects of selling with them, or convincing them that what they are experiencing can be turned around. In most cases, training members of this group is conducted individually or in a small group of associates who are experiencing similar situations. Sales managers typically do most or all of this training because they must be fully involved to help the associates begin to change what they are doing.

The third group needs little training yet cannot be forgotten. They are the experienced, successful sales associates who are doing well. While they do not need much in the way of training, they still must be kept aware of company/office changes, involved in sales team activities, and congratulated on their successes. You may want to enlist them to help with parts of your training program. This not only gives them positive recognition, it provides them with a form of self-training that can reinforce what works for them.

The final group is associates who have been in the business for a while and who have not been and currently are not productive. Chances are no amount of training will change their performance. As a result, a career adjustment is probably the best mutual solution.

Another approach to determining groups that have common training needs is called quartiling. With this approach you divide your associates into four groups based on units (sales and listings) closed, dollar volume closed, units or dollar volume under agreement, and associate earnings.

The division into four groups does not have to be exactly equal. It is more important to rank the associates by performance. For example, if an office has 16 associates, their six-month, closed-commission personal earnings might look like this:

Laurie	$32,500
Mark	30,000
Karen	28,700
Linda	27,800
Steve	26,900
Julie	23,000
Joe	21,000
Helen	19,200
Kathy	15,000
Joan	13,400
Sally	11,000
Tom	6,500
Cindy	4,000
Ann	1,800
Judy	1,700
Dennis	500

The first five associates, based on their similar earnings, can be grouped together. The next three associates fit together well, as do the last two groups of three and five. The four groups do not need to have equal numbers of associates.

Excluding any undisclosed special circumstances, groups two and three probably have room to grow from a personal production standpoint. Exceptions may include an associate who had a lucky big transaction or one who was in the top quartile and now is sliding backwards. The top group, in most cases, probably needs little skill development, leaving knowledge and attitude as their only real areas of need. Their knowledge needs usually can be satisfied with update sessions or sales meetings; their attitude needs can be fulfilled by recognizing their accomplishments both privately and publicly.

The last group usually contains an assortment of associates, including some new to the business, some who have fallen from higher groups, and some who always have resided at the bottom. This group probably will need both group and individual training to help them move up or out of the organization.

By analyzing each of these groups, you will be able to determine their specific training needs. Combined with company/office needs, you now have the basis to begin developing your training program. One note of caution: Within each of the groups described you may find individuals who need special help. They may or may not benefit from group sessions. Only you, with their input, can determine what will have the most potential impact on making them productive.

Finally, in determining training needs, use this set of questions to help zero in on specific needs:

1. Who is having problems? (Could be an individual or a group.)
2. What specific areas of selling/listing are they having problems with?
3. Is the problem a skill deficiency? If so, were they ever able to perform the skill? (Examples: The inability to obtain appointments from telephone call-ins; a lack of success in closing sellers during listing appointments.)
4. Is the problem a lack of knowledge? Not fully understanding new financing programs or not knowing what contingency clauses to use in a purchase agreement are examples of knowledge problems.
5. Is their attitude a problem? Evidence of attitude problems can include being late to meetings and for floor time, complaining about market conditions, and repeatedly finding fault with buyers and sellers.
6. Is the company or office losing production? If so, how much and in what area?
7. Is the problem important to the smooth operation of the company/office?
8. Do your sales associates know what is expected of them?
9. Is the problem caused by the company/office?
10. Are you the cause of the problem?

One effective method of answering questions related to actual versus perceived needs is to use tracking devices. Tracking can be performed on a day-to-day basis or in conjunction with specific company/office activities, such as sales contests or games.

If one of your company/office objectives is to increase sales, then you must increase the "pro-active" selling activities of your associates that lead to sales. If you set up a system of tracking activities as well as sales results, you will be able to pinpoint the specific training needs of individuals or small groups. By setting up a system for tracking selling activity with your associates, you will be highlighting areas that they must do well in to be successful at selling. You will also be improving your ability to coach associates on their individual selling needs.

Each week or once a month, a report can be completed showing the amount of activity by each associate in each category. If an associate held three open houses, conducted four buyer-qualification appointments, and showed 45 properties with no offers to purchase, obviously the associate has a problem. The manager can counsel the associate, determine the associate's areas of need, and conduct individual training sessions with the associate. Or, if a number of associates seem to be having similar problems, the manager can organize a small group for a training session. This also can prove helpful from an overall company standpoint. The general training program can be assessed, possibly revealing areas that need to be changed. Or the need for a company-wide special training program can be determined.

Activity tracking can also be used to set up a sales game or contest by awarding a differing number of points for each category. At the end of the game/contest period, the points are totaled and prizes awarded. Different prizes could be "won" for achieving specific point levels, or a drawing could be held for a prize with a person's name being put into the drawing for each point, or an auction could be held with the points being used as money for the bidding. Two tracking forms (one for listings, one for sales) are found on pages 23 and 24. Together they illustrate one way to set up a tracking system. By tracking activity using a sales game or contest, you can stimulate sales and determine training needs.

A carefully completed needs analysis forms the foundation for your company's program—whether it will be for new or experienced associates, done in groups or with individuals, completed in a single session or after a series of sessions, etc. Using what you have learned from your needs analysis will provide you with the necessary information to begin the actual development of your training program, which is establishing objectives.

Listing Activity

Associate _____

Month _____

Week	Pro-active Contact	Reactive Contact	Initial/ CMA Appt.	Presen. Appt.	Listings Obtained	Listings Not Obtained	Referrals Sent
Month's Totals							

Notes: A week runs from Monday through Sunday

Pro-active Contact Codes: FSBO – For Sale By Owners; E – Expired; F – Farm; S – Sphere of Influence; C – Canvassing; H – Open House; O – Other

Reactive Contact Codes: A – Ad Call; S – Sign Call; O – Other

Selling Activity

Associate _____

Month _____

Week	Pro-active Contact	Reactive Contact	Qualif. Appt.	Showings	Offers to Pur. Written	Offers Accepted	Offers Rejected	Showings to UA Ratio	P&S Agreements	Referral Sent
Month's Totals										

Notes: A week runs from Monday through Sunday

Pro-active Contact Codes: F – Farm; S – Sphere of Influence; C – Canvassing;
H – Open House; O – Other

Reactive Contact Codes: A – Ad Call; S – Sign Call; O – Other

4

Establishing Training Objectives

Objectives set the direction for your training program and should attempt to satisfy the needs uncovered by your needs analysis. Your objectives establish what material must be covered, when the material should be presented, what equipment to use, and how you will determine the success of your efforts. Basically, your objectives should answer three questions:

1. What will my sales associates learn and what will they be able to do as a result of the training?
2. What has to be taught and practiced to enable them to learn and perform the necessary skills?
3. How will you and they be able to determine whether they have learned the skills and can perform them?

General and Specific Objectives

It is important that you recognize the two basic types of objectives: general and specific. Your ability to use objectives effectively to develop and present your training program and to measure results will depend in part on your understanding of these two types of objectives.

General learning objectives, or general training objectives, are broad in nature and set the stage for establishing specific objectives. The goal of increasing listings by 20 percent over a previous time period is an example of a general objective. To try and develop training from this type of objective probably would prove to be very frustrating because it covers such a vast range of knowledge and skills.

To make general objectives more manageable, the steps to obtaining listings can be outlined. From this outline specific objectives can be created. If the first step in obtaining listings is to find sellers who want to sell, specific objectives could be written as follows:

As a result of this training session, the participants will be able to:

- List sources of potential listings
- Describe sales tools and dialogue to be used when approaching prospective listings
- Demonstrate an approach to at least one source

Notice the use of certain words in the objectives. "As a result of" is the lead-in for the specific areas that will be used to judge how successfully the associates complete the training program. The word "participants" indicates that the associates are not passive observers. Remember, training deals with the "doing" process. To be able to "do," the associates must be actively involved and must practice the skill being taught. The phrase "be able to" indicates that the associates will be able to do something or, in other cases, will know or feel something from going through the training.

The words used are important. "List," "describe" and "demonstrate" are words that say the participants will be able to perform certain tasks. If "know," "understand" and "realize" are used, the focus is on imparting knowledge, which is an educational function and only part of the overall training function. You should use words that describe what the participants will be able to do as a result of their training, not as a result of actual selling activity.

This one example is only a small part of the process of obtaining a listing. Many more objectives must be written to cover the numerous steps involved. While this may seem like quite a task, it really is not that difficult if you first outline the major elements or steps of the listing process. The dividend to you for the time invested is that your participants will have a clear view of both the overall objective and the specific skills and knowledge necessary for success. It is much easier to take one step at a time to reach a goal than to try a running leap and wind up falling short.

When preparing your objectives, keep your real goals in mind:

- What the participants must know and be able to do
- What they should know and be able to do
- What they might like to know and be able to do
- What you feel would be helpful for them to know and be able to do

Your primary goal is to train the participants in what they must know and be able to do to be successful. Once this is accomplished, you can cover what they should know and be able to do to maximize their potential for success. Covering what they would like to hear and what you feel would be helpful can round out the training so long as they have the basic information and skills, and you have the time.

Now that needs have been determined and objectives established, budget estimates can be made.

5

Budgeting Considerations

Like any type of budgeting, establishing a budget for training can be simple or complex. Many elements will affect the size of your training budget, such as the results of your needs analysis, your objectives, the number of associates to be trained at a time, the equipment and training materials that need to be obtained, and the competitive forces in your marketplace.

A problem with budgeting for training is where to place the budgeting process in the steps to developing a training program. The easiest place is at the beginning. Establish right away the amount of money available for training. This way, regardless of needs, objectives, and economic and competitive factors, you know exactly how much you can spend. In an ideal world, this might work.

A second place to do the budgeting is at the end. The problem with this approach is that after you have completed all the work on your training program, you may discover that you do not have the necessary dollars to complete the project as developed. The best idea is to tackle budgeting after you've established your training objectives. At this point you should be able to make a fairly accurate estimate of how much money you'll need to achieve the desired results. Regardless of your company size, budgeting at this stage can work very well, especially just prior to the beginning of your fiscal year. By reviewing the past 12 months, determining what was accomplished and what it cost, and analyzing needs for the next 12 months, you can arrive at a good estimate. While this works well for new-associate training and for prescheduled, experienced-associate training, you also should create a contingency training budget so you will be prepared for changes in your company, office and marketplace.

There are four basic approaches to establishing a training budget and three main cost areas associated with training that must be considered during the budgeting process. These are discussed in the next two sections.

Approaches to Budgeting

• **Past Experience and Actual Results.** As indicated previously, this approach involves a review of how much was spent during the previous year and an evaluation of the results. When using this approach, you assume that your needs will not vary much in the coming year. As with all budgeting, you should build in a contingency amount in case you run into unexpected circumstances that necessitate additional training or substantial revisions to your current training program.

• **Task Approach.** As the name implies, this involves determining what must be done. This approach combines your needs analysis and training objectives. For example, if one of your company objectives is to recruit a certain number of associates within a given time frame, you must have the resources available to train them. As stated in a previous chapter, your associates are your primary contacts with the public and must be prepared to do a good job.

• **Percentage of Company Dollars.** This approach can either be used alone or in combination with another approach. When used alone, a percentage of company dollars is designated for training, either arbitrarily or based on past experience. Combined with another approach, company-dollar percentages can be used to set a cap on the amount of the budget used for training. For example, if the task approach is used to arrive at a training budget, the amount then can be compared with the percentage allocated for training from the company's overall budget. If the task-approach amount is higher than desired in relationship to the other budget items, it can be revised to fall within the desired range.

The Economics Department of the NATIONAL ASSOCIATION OF REALTORS® periodically publishes reports that indicate expenses as a percentage of company dollars for different sizes and types of real estate companies. You can use this information as a guide to establish your own budget. However, the data should be used only as a guide because many factors will influence actual percentages. Just because the reports show an amount for training does not mean you should set yours the same. Some companies overspend, others have special needs, and still others have different objectives.

• **Competitive Parity.** This approach should be used with caution, because your competitors may approach budgeting in ways completely different from your own. Your competitors may overspend, or they may have special needs or objectives. You must know what other companies are doing so you can stay competitive. But staying competitive can be accomplished in many ways besides spending as much as or more than the competition.

Cost Areas

• **Development Costs.** These could include any or all of the following: The cost to develop a company training program in house (which usually is not great unless you pay someone to develop the material for you); the cost to purchase prepackaged or on-the-shelf programs (which can cost from a few dollars to several thousand, depending on the program); the cost to modify or customize prepackaged programs so they will better fit your organization (which normally involves adding specifics about your company, office procedures, the Multiple Listing Service, economic conditions, financing options and market area, including company sales and promotional tools); and the cost to develop and produce support materials, such as slides, overhead transparencies, handouts and training outlines.

• **Presentation Costs.** These include all costs related to the actual training session, such as the training room (rented or existing space), refreshments, special audio/visual equipment (rented or purchased), miscellaneous supplies, and speakers (either salaried employees or paid outside speakers).

• **Follow-up Costs.** These include all costs associated with any follow-up measures that are part of the training program, such as immediate evaluations of just-completed sessions, individualized follow-ups to the original training session that reinforce what was learned, and studies that measure the overall effectiveness of the program in achieving company production objectives. Unless an outside person is hired to perform these tasks, the actual costs can be minimized. Most of the costs involve the time spent by a manager and/or a secretary.

Unfortunately, no magic formula can be used to determine training costs. Your costs will depend on your needs and objectives and how elaborate you want your training to be. As illustrated in a previous example, training can improve associate effectiveness and productivity, which leads to bigger profits. When determining how much you are willing to spend on training, bear in mind the high cost of poorly or inadequately trained associates. What you actually spend for training probably will appear to be a very wise and cost-effective investment.

6 Selecting and Organizing Content

Selecting and organizing content is probably the most challenging step in developing a training program. You need to determine how much content there should be, how complex to make it, and how to organize it. As with the other steps in the development process, part of the answer lies in your needs analysis and objectives. In addition, the knowledge level of the trainers and of the participants will play a large role in determining what material you present, as will the particular topics to be covered in the various sessions.

Recall from our earlier discussion that training consists of three areas: knowledge, skill and attitude. Training associates to correctly complete listing and purchase agreements will require heavy emphasis on knowledge, for example. While skill development also will be required, much of what you will cover will involve the participants understanding how to complete the documents.

Telephone canvassing, however, requires more skill than knowledge. Therefore your training approach needs to acknowledge this. After all, good communication makes a big difference in how successful associates are at obtaining appointments or leads.

Attitude is subjective and really encompasses the other two areas. Associates must feel good about what they are doing and must possess a positive outlook on the results they will achieve. Many factors can influence attitude. If the associates possess the knowledge they are supposed to and can perform the various activities using their selling skills, their overall attitude will be positive. Thus, skill practice and positive reinforcement and feedback are critical to helping associates establish and maintain their positive outlook. Using an occasional "motivational" speaker or audio/visual program can provide added stimulation, although the effects normally are short-lived.

If a general objective of a listing-process training session is to explain and demonstrate the steps necessary to obtain a marketable listing, what are the components of the knowledge, skill and attitude areas that must be included?

33

Knowledge:

a. Sources of listings
b. Dialogue to use when prospecting
c. Dialogue necessary to obtain a listing presentation appointment
d. Data needed to prepare for the listing appointment and complete a market analysis
e. Methods to complete a market analysis, including establishing a possible or recommended listing price range
f. Items to take on a listing appointment
g. Format to follow during a listing presentation; general and key points to cover
h. When and how to close
i. How to recognize and handle objectives
j. How to complete a listing agreement/contract

Skills:

a. Using prospecting dialogue
b. Using dialogue to obtain an appointment
c. Completing a market analysis and listing price-range recommendation using data gathered
d. Making a listing presentation, including asking questions and listening for feedback
e. Asking for the order
f. Handling objections
g. Correctly completing a listing agreement/contract

Attitude:

a. Working in groups to discuss knowledge and to develop ways to use it throughout the process
b. Performing assignments covering market analysis completion, compiling materials for appointments, and filling out listing agreements
c. Role-playing steps in the listing process that involve associate and seller interaction

Note: Attitude is indirectly affected. The more associates practice an activity, the better they will understand the process and be able to successfully perform it. As their comfort level with each area of selling rises, their attitude, confidence and feelings about what they are doing will improve. Even though all of this is conducted in a safe training environment, associates still will be much better prepared to handle the realities in the field.

You may want to add items to or delete items from these lists. However, the point is that the content of your training program will depend on how much you want to cover and how complex you want it to be, your audience's level of understanding and skill, the trainer's level of understanding and skill, and your company's general and specific needs.

Organizing the content can be accomplished in many ways. The following three methods should serve all your needs.

- **Simple to Complex.** These three words say it all. You begin by using the most basic information and skill practice techniques to form a base. Then, like building blocks, you add a piece at a time until you have built a complete and often complex structure. This is the method you probably will use most often, and it is the one that seems to work best for sales.

- **Sequential.** Many of the selling activities in real estate follow a certain order. Selling a house progresses from the initial contact through qualifying, showing, etc., to the eventual closing. In most instances, to leap from one step to another step several links down the chain can lead to no sale or to a sale with ongoing problems right through closing. Thus, organizing your material in a sequential format helps to explain and reinforce the "right" way to carry out the selling activity in which you are involved.

- **General to Specific.** This method involves providing the participants with an overview of the subject area before covering the specifics. Using this method in combination with either of the first two methods helps prepare the participants for what they will be doing.

In addition to providing a clear, understandable beginning, the general overview approach can be used to summarize material during and at the end of the training session. This helps the participants keep the detailed information in perspective with the "big picture."

Most of your time will be spent planning the content and organization of your program. Often individuals involved in training will spend four to six hours preparing for each hour of actual presentation time. Do not let these times throw you. How much time you spend will depend on your knowledge and skill levels, plus the subject matter you will be covering. The key is thorough and complete preparation. Once the content is just the way you want and need it to be, the actual presentation will seem much easier.

7 Selecting Equipment and Materials

You do not have to use audio/visual aids with every part of your training program, yet they can greatly enhance what you do.

Studies have shown that using audio/visual aids stimulates the sense of hearing and seeing which, in turn, improves learning and recall. When people only hear something, they can recall about 70 percent of what was heard three hours later. This recall figure drops to about 10 percent after three days. If they only see something, they can recall about 72 percent three hours later and only about 20 percent three days later. By combining audio and visual, recall improves to about 85 percent after three hours and about 65 percent after three days! That's quite a difference from using audio or visual independently.

When deciding what audio/visual aids to employ, keep in mind the following considerations:

1. Are the aids more elaborate (and therefore more costly) than they need to be? Some professional speakers and instructors use very complete, colorful and fancy aids, especially visual ones. While these aids are great to use, virtually the same impact can be achieved using much simpler aids. You can always improve the quality of your visual aids over time if you want to.
2. Will the aids increase your effectiveness in achieving your training objectives? In most cases the answer will be "yes." In cases where using more than one aid will help achieve your objectives, you must weigh the cost factors to determine which aids to choose.
3. Are the aids appropriate for the group size and the training environment? Will everyone be able to adequately see and hear what you are presenting? The size, shape and construction of the room may prove to be more of a distraction than a help to your audience. It is very frustrating not to be able to see or hear. What could have been a big plus for the training session may become a negative that is hard to overcome.

4. Will the aids work well to support your training materials? The aids should increase the ability of the participants to achieve their training objectives. Using audio/visual aids just for the sake of using them sometimes can hinder rather than help.

5. Are the aids within your budget? Sometimes audio/visual aids can eat up a large portion of your budget. If this is the case, you may want to consider using less costly aids as long as they do not decrease the effectiveness of your presentation.

6. Are the aids portable? This becomes especially important if the aids must be returned to storage or used in different locations.

7. Are too many different aids being used? When trying to maximize the impact of training, trainers may use too many audio, visual, and audio/visual elements. This can diminish the effectiveness and benefits derived from using aids. This also is true if you are using only one piece of equipment. If you are using an overhead projector and show 45 transparencies in an hour, you probably will lose most of your audience. The presentation becomes too much for them to see, hear and absorb. A better approach is to use fewer slides and only the ones that emphasize your key points; 10 to 12 can work well. The exception might be if you quickly show examples (pictures) of materials such as promotional items. Even so, caution must be exercised so that you do not try to cover too much material during a short period of time.

Following is a list of training aids you can use. Costs are not included because they will vary greatly from market to market and will depend on the types and quality of equipment you purchase. When acquiring training aids such as audiocassette players, VCRs and overhead projectors, you should comparison shop at several different suppliers to obtain the best prices possible.

• **Writing Boards.** These are the least-expensive and simplest aids to employ. They include chalkboards and "white" boards. Chalkboards, other than being used in schools, generally have been replaced by white boards. White boards can be written on with a number of colored markers, are easy to read and easy to clean up.

• **Flip Charts.** Flip charts can be used almost anywhere by hanging them on wall pegs or by using an easel. The paper comes in pads and is available through most office-supply and art stores. The cost of the pads is quite low, although a good-quality easel can cost several hundred dollars.

This is a great aid to employ with smaller groups when you want to stress key points or develop ideas during a presentation. You can even prepare in advance by writing out your key points prior to the training session. If you use this approach, leave a blank piece of paper between each sheet that has writing on it. This way you can flip a sheet you already have discussed without uncovering the next sheet until you are ready.

• **Handout Materials.** These materials are given to the participants to reinforce what has been covered or is about to be covered. They usually are relatively inexpensive and very easy to use. The key consideration is timing. Unless the audience needs the materials, don't hand them out until you reach the point in your presentation where you will refer to them. Otherwise the participants may spend part of their time looking through what you have handed out and may not pay attention to what you are trying to say.

• **Overhead Projectors and Transparencies.** By using this type of projector, you can maintain face-to-face contact while you are displaying the visual aid to the group. The overhead projector is easy to use (although you should practice a bit) and requires only normal room lighting. Using an overhead projector helps focus the attention of the participants and allows you to make on-the-spot changes in your presentation. For example, if you find that because of the participants' level of understanding or the speed with which they are grasping the material that you must change your presentation, you can do so simply by rearranging or deleting transparencies. In addition, you can use blank transparencies to add points or to give examples as the need arises. While a good-quality overhead projector can be expensive, it will last a long time and enable you to greatly enhance your training sessions.

Transparencies are available in different types to fill almost every need. The most common transparency is designed to be run through an ordinary photocopier, where it reproduces the image that appears on the master. If the copier reproduces in color, the transparencies can be reproduced in color as well. There are also special transparency machines that can print transparencies in one or more colors. Your office-supply store or audio/visual equipment supplier can provide you with all the necessary information. In addition, 3-M provides brochures that cover various methods of creating transparencies. Transparencies, depending on the type, are not inexpensive when used in large quantities; so plan well for their production and use.

When presenting a series of key points on a single transparency, you can place a sheet of paper over or under the transparency to block the projection of the printed material. As you mention each point, you simply slide the paper down to reveal the printed information. When changing transparencies, turn the projector off unless you are rapidly showing a series of examples. Stand to either side of the projector so you do not block the projection light or the screen. One final comment: Speak to your audience, not to the screen.

A good learning method is to observe how others use overhead projectors, transparencies, and other audio/visual equipment. You can build on what you feel works best and watch for potential problem areas to eliminate.

• **Screens.** When using screens, try to follow the "two-by-six rule" for screen placement. According to this rule, the front row of participants should not be closer than two times the width of the screen and the last row of participants should not be further away than six times the width of the screen. In addition, you should be sure that the size of the prints or illustrations can be seen by everyone. To check this, project a sample of what you will be using and walk around the room to determine the material's visibility. Be sure that the projector, podium and other equipment do not block the view of any of the participants.

- **Audiocassette Players and Tapes.** Because audiocassettes engage only one sense—hearing—they are not the best aid for group training. Individuals have very short attention spans, and when they are required to sit and listen to a tape with nothing else going on around them, they may drift off very quickly.

The best use for audiocassette players and tapes is individual listening. Tapes can be listened to in the office (with earphones), in the car, in the home, or just about anyplace. While many tapes offer detailed information, much of it will sail right over the heads of individuals who listen only once and are not prepared to take notes. Repeated listening can correct part of this problem. Probably the best tapes to use are those that present a fairly general message with a few well-illustrated key points or those that are designed to be stimulating and motivational.

- **VCRs, Televisions and Videotapes.** Because of the rapidly changing nature of VCRs and televisions, your selection and cost will vary. One point to keep in mind is that both are available in consumer and commercial models. For the typical company or office training program, you probably can use consumer-grade equipment. For frequent use, even though the cost is higher, commercial-grade equipment may be better. Two big advantages of using these types of aids are that the equipment normally is fairly simple to operate and that unlike film and slides, the room lighting can be left in its normal setting for viewing programs, although slightly lowering the lights does help viewing somewhat.

Videotapes are available either as prepackaged learning programs or blank tapes. Programmed materials are excellent if prepared and used correctly. A wide variety currently is on the market. If you buy a preprogrammed videotape series, be sure it includes adequate written support materials that instruct you on how to conduct the program. Ideally, printed materials for the participants also should be available so that exercises, basic information and notes are already printed out for them. This will greatly enhance the training experience. *The Real Estate Success Series** is one program that provides complete support materials for the trainer and program participants.

Blank videotapes can be used to record participants in role-play situations. They can provide valuable feedback. Two areas of caution: First, many people do not want to role play in front of a group and this reluctance may be increased when a camera is present. Second, do not

---

The Real Estate Success Series is a comprehensive sales associate video training program, developed and distributed by the Real Estate Brokerage Council™, of the REALTORS NATIONAL MARKETING INSTITUTE®, an affiliate of the NATIONAL ASSOCIATION OF REALTORS®.

play back the tape for the group. At most, you and the individual participants should view the tape. For evaluation, ask the participants what they thought about their performance and what they would do differently the next time. Your comments should follow and should reinforce the positive aspects of what they did.

- **Films and Slides.** While both of these aids can provide useful information, they do require that you darken the room for good viewing. They also tend to be somewhat inflexible, as it is difficult to rearrange the order of slides or to advance/rewind films.

These factors should not stop you from considering using them. There are good programs available on slides (including slide/audiocassette programs) and film. However, before making the decision to purchase a slide or film program, you may want to check to see if it is available on videotape as well.

- **Books.** Books can provide excellent reinforcement for the information covered in your training program, though many people will not take the time to read them. To maximize the benefits for those who do, a review session should be conducted where the participants can discuss what they have read and how it might be applied to the real estate sales business.

- **Training Manuals.** At the very least, your participants should receive an outline of each session, including the training objectives and the key points that will be covered in the order that you plan to cover them. This will help the participants take notes and follow what is presented.

Ideally you should give them a manual that contains most, if not all, of the details you will cover. Putting such a manual together involves a good deal of time and effort on your part. Because your overall training goal is to shape your associates' behavior in order to positively influence how they sell, providing a complete manual allows you and your associates to focus on skill development because the knowledge portion already is laid out for them in writing. Because of the time and work involved, you may find that it is better to build your manual over time, adding sections as they are finished. As an alternative, you may want to consider using a prepackaged program or a basic book on selling. Even though you may need to adapt and customize these, much of the basic information probably will be covered.

Regardless of what aids you choose, make every effort to accompany them with as much specific printed information as possible.

As stated previously, audio/visual aids can do much to enhance your training program. Which aids you use will depend on what you are trying to present and on your budget. Remember, with audio/visual aids something usually is better than nothing. As the saying goes, "A picture is worth a thousand words."

8 Determining Trainers and Training Methods

You have put a lot of effort into your training program to this point without presenting it to or involving your sales associates. This is the way it should be. Thorough preparation will make the actual presentation easier for you and more beneficial to the participants. Before discussing the training environment, scheduling the material and presenting the material, it is necessary to examine who the trainer should be.

Trainer Characteristics

Trainer, instructor, sales manager—whatever the title, this person is the most vital element of your training program. You can offer clear objectives, the best equipment and outstanding material and your program still could fail because of an unprepared, unmotivated, uninterested trainer. On the other hand, a good trainer can transform weak material into meaningful information for program participants. Trainers do not have to be great speakers. If they possess the characteristics in the following list, they should be able to do a good job.

• **Knowledge.** A complete understanding of the material to be covered is important. This does not mean that you, as the trainer, must have all the answers. But you should be able to give an in-depth presentation of the material and be able to answer most questions. In the rare cases when a question is asked that you do not have a ready answer for, just indicate that you are not sure of the answer and that you will research the matter and get back to the participants.

One further key consideration: Knowledge is great only if it is presented clearly and understandably to the audience. Do not try to complicate the subject; keep it simple and stay with the essentials.

• **Communication Skills.** Great knowledge is worthless unless it can be communicated. Good training communication is a two-way process. You must be able to get the information across and demonstrate necessary skills, and you must be sure that the participants receive the information and can perform the skills. Near the end of this chapter is a list of training hints. The key is that your communication must be two-way.

• **People Skills.** This ties in with communication. Your sales associates must know that you care about their expectations, concerns and frustrations. As with selling, people do not care how much you know or can do until they know how much you care about them. Even with good people skills you will encounter problem individuals. Try to deal with these participants in private. Using sarcasm or ridicule or talking down to a participant may release some of your frustrations and even get a laugh from many of the other participants. Yet in the long run you will lose something in their eyes.

• **Self-Image.** Visualizing yourself giving an effective and interesting presentation, achieving group involvement and accomplishing your training objectives will lead you and your group to a successful and worthwhile outcome. Without a positive self-image, you will have a much harder time attaining good results from your training.

• **Confidence.** Good speakers appear to be confident about themselves and about the material they are teaching. This does not mean they are not nervous. Being nervous is a natural reaction to speaking publicly, and even experienced speakers become nervous before a presentation. Being well-prepared is the best way to develop a sense of confidence. If you are prepared, you can turn your nervous energy into a positive force that will help drive your presentation.

• **Humor.** You do not have to be a comedian to be a good trainer. This is a good thing, since most people are not comedians. By simply smiling you can help the group to relax. Humor drawn from funny personal experiences or the experiences of others works best. It helps reinforce key points in the material and makes the training experience more enjoyable. If you do tell jokes, be careful not to overdo them and be sure they relate to what you are discussing.

• **Credibility.** You do not always have to be a proven expert with complete actual experience to be able to deliver material on a certain subject. While having a lot of experience in the subject you are covering is desirable, being totally prepared often will overcome any lack of experience. For example, new sales associates have no experience to share with the first sellers to whom they make a presentation. Yet being fully prepared to discuss market conditions, the market analysis on the sellers' home, what the company can and will do to help sell their home, etc., does lead to listings.

- **Enthusiasm.** This is the most important characteristic. Without enthusiasm, all the rest will fall short. If you are not enthusiastic and interested in what you are doing, the program participants will not be either.

With the key characteristics outlined, who then are the possible trainers? In general, trainers should be knowledgeable about what is to be taught and should be able to effectively communicate. He or she should be able to get participants involved and bring about the desired results. Your obligation to your sales associates is to select the best trainers available. If the best trainer is you, go for it!

Another way to look at this is demonstrated by the figure below, which is a square divided into four communication and teaching styles.

Trainers who fall into the upper-left quarter mainly are concerned with the material and often with themselves. As a result, they tend to lecture the participants and at times even talk down to them. While the participants are likely to develop some limited knowledge, this lecturing style does not develop skills and can negatively affect attitudes.

Trainers who fall into the lower-left quarter probably do not even want to be there. They will exhibit little or no interest and enthusiasm and, as a result, nothing much will take place except a waste of everyone's time.

The lower-right quarter is represented by trainers who want everyone to have a good time. They usually have a high-level need to be liked by the people they teach. While they may realize that the material to be covered is important, their major thrust is to have everyone feel good about the training experience and about them. Some learning and skill development may result, yet not to the degree desired. The attitude of the participants over the short term will be positive. But as they begin to realize that they did not gain much from the training experience, their attitude may change.

The upper-right quarter consists of trainers who understand the importance of the material and the importance of the participants. These trainers make every effort to convey the necessary information

	One-way Communication — Lecture	Two-way Communication — Interact/Involve
Importance of Material	Miscommunication — Wander	Partial Communication — Amuse

Importance of Trainees
*To Correct Print Error

while obtaining ongoing feedback and participation. They recognize and appreciate the participants and make every effort to achieve the training objectives with the participants' active involvement.

A variety of people can make excellent trainers, including:

- Broker/owners
- Branch/sales managers (in multiple-office companies this could be the manager from the same office as the participants or a manager from a different office)
- Sales associates
- Outside "experts"
- Trainers lent through a cooperative training arrangement with competitors (usually arranged through a local board of REALTORS®)

A word of caution: When employing outside trainers to conduct all or part of your training program, be sure they are absolutely clear on what you want them to cover, how you would like it covered, and how long they have to cover it. Most trainers appreciate the guidance and you will achieve better results.

Training Environment

Where you conduct your training is important. Depending on your budget, you may be able to use a separate space or facility for training. Or you may have to allocate a portion of your sales office or a personal office. Regardless of where you conduct your training, try to meet as many of the following criteria as possible. This will benefit everyone involved with the program— trainers and participants alike— and will greatly help you to achieve your training objectives.

- **No Interruptions or Distractions.** It is critical that you try to provide a training environment where the group will not be disturbed by people walking in and out, telephones ringing, outdoor distractions, etc. If you must conduct training where the telephone is going to ring or where there will be interruptions, then assign at least one person to cover the telephone and other interruptions so the rest of the group is not overly disturbed. Also, it is helpful if your training area is free of clutter and unneeded materials. Try to schedule your training at a time when there will be the fewest potential distractions.

- **Visibility.** Your training area should be set up so that you and any materials you will be using can easily be seen by the group. In most cases you will be standing and your materials will be placed at a height visible to everyone. This helps you control and facilitate the learning process.

- **Temperature.** You can't please all of the people all of the time. Try to keep the training area cool. If it gets too warm, people will have trouble focusing their attention. Some may even fall asleep. Maintaining a temperature from 68 to 70 degrees seems to work best for most groups.

- **Lighting.** A well-lit room improves training by making everything more visible and reducing eye fatigue. Natural light from the outside is good except that you cannot control the brightness or in some cases the heat it generates. For best results use indoor lighting. Lighting contractors or space planners are good sources for information on lighting.

- **Ceiling Height.** If you have the freedom to select a room for your training, pick one with a high ceiling—at least 10 to 12 feet tall. This will improve your ability to effectively use various types of visual-projection equipment. Group size and the type of equipment you plan to use will affect the required ceiling height for your training program. The key is to make sure everyone can see what you are doing.

- **Room Color.** If possible, use an area that is decorated in light colors. Light colors brighten an area and makes it easier for people to see what is happening. They also can enhance your lighting.

- **Seating.** There are several suggested seating arrangements. Review the type of learning and skill development that you want to take place. Each configuration has advantages and disadvantages depending on what you hope to accomplish. Also, to some extent the seating arrangement will be determined by the area you will be using for your training.

Chevron is the traditional classroom setup for large groups. The tables are slightly angled so that everyone can see the center of the front of the room without having to turn. Chevron is an excellent room setup for lectures. It also works fairly well for participative learning. The biggest disadvantage is that it tends to limit the amount of dialogue and interchange between the participants because they all are facing forward. Still, chevron is a good way to set up a room because it does work well. It also is quite flexible because it can fit into just about any type of space.

A *circle* arrangement is excellent for small groups where you want a lot of verbal interchange. It can be useful when you are presenting a limited amount of material and want the group to maximize discussion time. As the trainer, you need to be aware that you will lose much of your control because you probably will be in a seated position and therefore not the focal point you would be if you were standing at the front of the room.

The *horseshoe* setup is similar to the circle except that it is open at one end. This allows you to maintain control because you can make your presentation from the open space. The horseshoe also affords you space to set up your audio/visual equipment. When using this type of setup for an extended period of time, many of the participants may begin to get stiff necks because they will be sitting with their bodies and necks turned to view the information you are presenting. The horse-shoe is good mainly for short presentations and it does help to establish and maintain dialogue among the participants.

Roundtable is a good setup for small group discussions and can be used with all types of presentation methods. However, if you are going to be making presentations from the front of the room, position the participants around the table so that they are at least facing semi-forward to the front. It is very awkward for people to watch and listen, let alone participate, when they are sitting with their backs to the action.

The chief considerations for your training location are lack of interruptions, temperature control, and visibility. If you can control these conditions, then your seating arrangement and your audio/visual aids should work fine and your training location should maximize the potential for learning and skill development.

Scheduling

When to conduct training and for how long will depend mostly on who is doing the training. For example, if your trainers are also your sales managers, they probably will not be able to allocate large blocks of time to conduct training. On the other hand, if you hire full- or part-time trainers to conduct your training sessions, time is not a problem. Following is a list of scheduling considerations. The right schedule for your program will depend on who will do the training, what material will be covered, and where the training will take place.

• **Full-Day Sessions.** This type of session adheres to the "once you get them, keep them" philosophy. While people may voice good intentions toward training and may work hard at the beginning of the sessions, they tend to drop out as the number of sessions increases. Full-day sessions held over a series of consecutive days allow you to cover the most material in the shortest period of time. Your chances of keeping participants interested are increased because they do not have much time for outside distractions between sessions.

Your ability to offer full-day sessions will depend on the trainer's other duties, if any. Another factor when considering whether to offer full-day sessions is that without time to apply what is being taught, information and skills can be forgotten if the training runs for too many days and weeks in a row. Holding breaks between major sections to allow for limited field application can be very beneficial.

If you use full days, attempt to schedule most of the passive activity, such as lectures, in the morning. After lunch the participants may not be as attentive as they are in the morning, so you need to involve them in skill development and other exercises. However, this does not mean scheduling only lecture sessions in the morning. You still will want to schedule some non-lecture training activities in the morning in order to keep the participants' interest at the highest level possible.

• **Half Days.** These sessions can be held consecutively or every other day. Besides the problem of getting the associates to return for each session, a second problem arises. What do participants do with all the time in between the classroom sessions? Without a strong program of reinforcement, involvement and assistance from the sales managers or someone else, the associates may tend to wander between sessions. A series of full-day sessions in combination with follow-up half days may be a good alternative.

When using half days, mornings seem to work best. This is the time when people are most alert. Afternoons are acceptable, but as mentioned earlier many people tend to experience a downtime mentally and physically after lunch. Evenings are not recommended because people usually will be tired from the day's activities. As a result, they will not be as attentive or responsive as might be desired.

• **Weekends.** Scheduling Saturday sessions is a possibility, although several disadvantages exist. Many people plan family activities on weekends. While associates may conduct a large part of their selling on weekends, many do not think of this as a time for training. Another disadvantage is that a week between training sessions is too long a period of time. Finally, depending on your training philosophy you may want to use the weekends for assignments or for having associates get out in the field to apply what they learned in the training sessions.

Scheduling will depend on your company, the facilities available, your training program's format and content, and who will be conducting the training. Overall, your goal should be to select the schedule that best enables you to fulfill your objectives.

Presentation Methods

Presentation or teaching methods are the means of delivery by which people learn. If your presentation methods do not impart knowledge and develop skills, no learning will take place. The following should be viewed from both the participant and the trainer viewpoints.

First, consider for a moment the word "participant." The words "student" and "trainee" tend to denote people who sit and attempt to absorb the vast wisdom of the expert (trainer). "Participant," on the other hand, indicates involvement. And only through involvement will maximum learning and skill development take place. Whether you view the people in your training program as participants or students is up to you, the trainer. But if you involve your sales associates, you will maximize their potential for greater profit.

As Confucius said:

"I hear and I forget,
I see and I remember,
I do and I understand."

Following are several presentation methods. Using more than one during a session will improve the presentation, keep the participants interested, and accomplish the training objectives.

• **Town Hall.** This method can be used to generate information such as group concerns, interests and expectations, within the scope of the specific objectives of the session. It also can be used at the beginning of a training program to develop an overview of concerns and expectations. The town-hall method involves active participation by the group. By allowing the participants to state their concerns, interests and expectations, you are offering them partial "ownership" in the material to be covered.

The trainer asks the group a question such as "What are your major concerns about prospecting for buyers?" The trainer may either ask for responses immediately or ask the participants to write down their answers. The resulting lists indicate what the participants' concerns are and serve as a means of developing additional objectives for the session. They also allow the trainer the opportunity to deal with concerns, interests or expectations that are inappropriate for the session.

A second question might be "What are the most frequent objections you are likely to receive from a seller?" By answering this question, the group becomes a resource for the session. The participants share their strongest concerns about the particular subject and in so doing may add items to the trainer's list of seller objections.

• **Lecture.** This presentation method primarily is one-way communication that works well to deliver a large amount of information in a short period of time. Lecture provides a passive experience for the audience. If participants feel that they want and need to know what is being covered, they will try to listen. If not, their involvement will be close to zero.

When used in conjunction with visual aids, verbal examples and stories, humor, and other presentation methods, lecture can be effective.

Another form of the lecture method is the participative lecture. With this method the instructor involves the group to a limited extent by asking questions and obtaining feedback. Some control of the group and some time may be lost, but this can prove worthwhile if a lengthy lecture is going to be presented.

• **Role Play.** Basically, this presentation method helps participants internalize the content. In other words, they are not just hearing the information, they actually are feeling and experiencing the material because they are involved in putting what they have heard to use. Role play allows sales associates to "act out" a situation or problem in a relatively safe environment—"relatively safe" because role-playing associates still must deal with the judgment and observations of their peers.

By role playing, participants can gain confidence in using the materials they have learned in other segments of the training program. Through this confidence-building, their skills will develop faster and be stronger. When they actually go out in the field to use their newly acquired skills and knowledge, their potential for success will be increased.

Role playing allows participants to learn by doing. They can watch someone else—the trainer or several other participants—do something, and then they can imitate what was done. This imitation can follow the viewing of a videotape or film as well. Participants also can learn through observation and feedback. They observe others using certain skills and knowledge and are involved in the feedback process of telling those people how they did. Role playing probably is the most critical presentation method in helping sales associates to develop new behavior.

Role playing can take two forms—structured and spontaneous. Structured role plays are ones that have been developed in advance with sets of circumstances, or scenarios. You may have one small group or several small groups act out the skills they have learned by using the scenario you have created. For example, in one scenario you could have the participants approach the owner of a home that has a For-Sale-By-Owner sign in the front yard. According to the scenario, the participants know that the home should be in a certain price range and that it is being offered at a higher price than is appropriate. Verbally, or preferably in writing, your scenario describes the neighborhood, the types of homes that comprise it, and the market activity. Plus you have set an objective for the participants. For example, their objective could be to obtain an appointment to return and make a listing presentation to the owner.

After setting up this structured role play, you can ask two or three people from the group to come up and go through the role play to demonstrate how it should be done. The advantage of this is that the entire group can see and analyze how the information you have covered can be applied in the field. One disadvantage is that it really only involves one person, the one who is playing the sales associate. Another is that it can be an embarrassing or stressful situation for the two or three people who are asked to perform in front of the entire group.

Use multiple-role plays when you want everyone to practice a skill. The advantage of multiple role plays, where you break a large group into smaller groups of two to three people, is that everyone is involved. The result is a wide variety of conclusions and decisions that lead to different ways of solving the same problem. This eliminates the embarrassment of individual participants being on display in front of the entire group. There are disadvantages, however. For instance, some of the groups may finish earlier than others, leaving them with time on their hands. Conversely, depending on the size of your overall group there may be little time for group discussion and analysis. In addition, as the trainer you may find it difficult at times to judge the quality of everyone's performance. This last difficulty can be overcome to some extent by having an observer, the "buyer" and the "seller" relate to the "sales associate" their reactions and feelings about what was accomplished.

Whether you use single- or multiple-role plays, be sure that you rotate the role of the sales associate so that everyone has the chance to perform the skills they are there to learn.

In spontaneous role play, the material is obtained directly from the group. For example, in your discussion of how to qualify buyers, someone from the group may ask an interesting question. Rather than answering yourself or having someone else in the group answer, you may want to structure a very simple role play where two or three people volunteer to try to work through the problem as though they actually were going through a qualification appointment. This is just another way of involving the participants in the training function rather than trying to answer all the questions by talking.

Three basic steps are involved in the role-playing process: the introduction and warm-up, the actual role play, and the evaluation.

During the *introduction and warm-up* you explain to the participants what they will be doing and get them interested in participating. During and prior to this step, you should do the following:

- Make sure that all participants have been exposed to the required knowledge or at least enough of it so that they will have the information necessary to be involved with the role play.
- Check to see that they have received adequate and realistic information, and whether the role play is structured or spontaneous.
- Carefully explain the instructions. Of all the various challenges to trainers, one of the greatest is to make certain that the participants understand the instructions before beginning an exercise.
- Make sure that your role-playing exercise is part of your training objectives.
- Use observers, if possible, to provide feedback.

During the *actual role play* you should watch for the following:

- The accuracy of the approach used by the players
- The vocabulary and mannerisms they use
- Knowledge of your company's products and services
- Their knowledge of your company and its procedures
- Their communication skills
- Their selling skills

If you are using a multiple-role play with a number of groups role playing at the same time, be sure your observers realize that they, too, should be looking for these elements. You may want to prepare and hand out a simple checklist of the key points for the observers to use.

The third step is evaluation. Let's say, for instance, that you are using multiple-role plays of three people—one as the sales associate, one as the buyer or seller, and one as an observer. The person playing the sales associate should evaluate his or her own performance first. Simply ask: "How did you feel about what you did and what would you do differently the next time?" Have them be as specific as possible, not just a general "okay." Then ask for the reaction of the person playing the seller or the buyer. And finally ask for the observer's comments. A key instruction for the evaluators is to offer positive comments. The person who acted the part of the sales associate most likely will know where he or she needs to improve without hearing it from anyone else. That person needs positive reinforcement.

Role playing can do much to initiate and reinforce behavioral change and skill practice. Using it well and often can make a huge difference in the results of your training program.

• **Task Group.** This presentation method is excellent for use with any sized group because it involves all of the participants in studying, exploring and providing solutions to given situations. This method allows each member of the group to express an opinion and to influence the other members in arriving at a common decision.

Task groups also take some of the pressure off the trainers as the role resources. This method is used when you want to develop substantial input from the participants; when you want them to solve a problem rather than you simply giving them the answer. The task-group method maximizes the use of resources and gets everyone involved. This, in turn, helps develop the participants' problem-solving abilities, which are essential to selling. When using a task-group exercise you should follow these steps:

- Describe the problem.
- State the objective of the exercise.
- Give specific instructions, including time elements.
- Divide the participants into groups, each with a leader and possibly a reporter.
- Call for or process the reports.

To make your job simpler, write down the instructions and hand them out. This eliminates any confusion that might arise.

For example, assume you have been talking about prospecting for listings and have discussed the various tools and items available both from your company and from the outside that can aid in this endeavor. For steps "a" and "b," state that the objective is for "the participants to be able to develop and describe the use of three listing prospecting tools including dialogue as the result of this exercise." For step "c," tell the participants that they are to develop at least three tools and describe how to use the tools with actual dialogue as if they were approaching a potential client, an FSBO, an expired listing, a sphere of influence, or an owner in their farm area. Tell them they will have _____ minutes to work on their report.

For step "d," divide the participants into manageable groups of three to seven people and tell them to select group leaders. During the exercise, you should move around the room to see how they are doing and to answer any questions. For step "e," ask for their reports. You may want to make brief comments after each report. When doing this, however, be careful because you may inadvertently "steal" material from a report yet to come.

• **Case Study.** This presentation method can use the task-group format or can be performed independently. It involves the use of prepared materials that contain a series of instructions and situations needing answers or solutions.

When used with a group, time must be allotted so each group member can read through the material and determine some answers on his or her own. The group should then discuss each person's answers or solutions and arrive at a group consensus.

Used individually, case studies can help determine a person's comprehension, understanding and ability to apply what has been presented. A simple case study could involve buyer qualification using a narrative to set the stage by briefly describing the buyer's needs, wants, financial ability to buy and other factors; a buyer-qualification form; and an estimated closing cost sheet. Specific instructions must be given and participants should understand the criteria by which they will be judged. The evaluation process does not have to be overly detailed as long as you and the participants achieve the desired results in understanding and ability.

• **Action Plan.** This presentation method is used to help the participants summarize what has been covered in a particular training segment and how they will use the training material in the field. An action plan should be in writing because it is the foundation for a commitment as to how the participants will use what they have learned. Because it is a plan of action, a time element must be included. An action plan answers the following questions:

- What must be accomplished?
- When must it be accomplished?
- How will it be accomplished?
- Who will accomplish it?
- How will the results be measured or judged?

• **Coaching.** While not a classroom presentation method, coaching is the key to applying what takes place in the training environment to the "playing field." It serves to guide, reinforce and modify actual selling activities performed by the sales associates. It also serves to correct selling techniques that could lead to poor results or no results at all.

A listing presentation is a good example of coaching. A new associate comes into contact with some people who want to sell their home. With the sales manager's guidance and support, the sales associate is able to obtain an appointment to make a listing presentation. Prior to that, the manager and the sales associate preview the home so the associate can conduct a complete market analysis and develop a plan on how to approach the sellers to secure the listing. Before arriving at the home to make the presentation, the manager decides with the sales associate who actually will make the presentation.

Depending on the sales associate's development and levels of skill and confidence, the manager may have the sales associate give the entire presentation or the manager may split the presentation with the associate. Together they go to the home, make the listing presentation, and obtain the listing. As soon as they leave the home, they discuss what happened. The manager should ask how the sales associate felt about the presentation appointment—regardless of who made it—and how it could be conducted differently in the future. The manager then should indicate how he or she felt about it and suggest changes that might make it better the next time, regardless of whether the listing was obtained.

Be sure to keep your comments positive and enthusiastic. The coaching function should continue until you feel the sales associate has the ability to succeed or fail alone. Coaching never really stops. Even star athletes need constant positive reinforcement and feedback on what they are doing right, as well as critiques of their mistakes if they are to continue leading the team to victory. Regardless of the level of performance of your sales associates, they all need some coaching. The key is to coach them based on their level of needs.

• **Involvement and Feedback.** As repeatedly stated in this book, involvement and feedback are extremely important. To assist you in getting as much involvement and feedback as possible, you must ask questions.

Basically, there are four types of questions you can ask:

- Overhead questions, which are asked of the group as a whole and generally answered by volunteers

Example: "What are the major sources of buyers?"

- Directed questions, which are directed at individuals

Example: "Mary, would you list the key areas that should be covered during a listing presentation?"

- Reversed questions, which are directed back to the asker

Example: (Trainer is asked) "What is a good way to establish a rapport with visitors to an open house?"
(Response to questioner) "Well, if you were visiting an open house being held by a real estate sales associate, what would make you feel welcome and comfortable?"

- Relayed questions, which are questions asked by one participant and directed to another.

Example: (Trainer is asked) "What type of properties should we use for sold comparables when doing our market analysis?"
(Response to questioner) "A good question, Frank. Sally,

you showed me your completed market analysis. How did
you select the sold properties you used for comparables?''

To make questions work for you, you should prepare several general and specific questions in advance of the session. Try to avoid questions that call for a simple yes or no response. You can do this by using why, what, when, where, who or how in your questions.

Questions can help you in several ways:

- They help to involve the group, especially when you are using the lecture method.
- They provide a means for you to judge whether the group understands the material. This, of course, is true only of participants responding to your questions, so you should try to get different people to answer each question.
- They draw out information and opinions.
- They focus attention on specific points.
- They help you control the discussion.

Questions are excellent tools for increasing involvement and obtaining feedback. Be careful, however, to not ask too many questions during any one session. There is no exact number that you should ask; you will have to gauge your audience and decide accordingly.

To obtain the most benefit from these various methods, you must use more than one. When used in combinations, they produce a much greater positive effect on the participants than when used separately.

Five Stages of Training

Each training session can be divided into five stages: preparation, presentation, application, examination/evaluation, and summary.

• **Preparation.** As mentioned previously, this includes developing clear training objectives, developing and organizing content, determining aids to be used, locating a training area, and scheduling. Without thorough preparation all else will fall short.

• **Presentation.** This is when training actually takes place. Using the methods previously described, a presentation can be broken down into three parts: introduction, explanation and demonstration.

During the *introduction* you set the stage, get the participants' attention, and let them know what to expect. The introduction need not be lengthy, just long enough to get the session off to a good start.

The *explanation* is where you begin to fulfill the promise of the introduction. Your goal is to provide participants with the information necessary to perform the skills being developed. During the explanation you should use examples, ask questions and conclude each discussion with a brief summary. Above all, keep it simple.

In the third part, you (or someone else) give a *demonstration* of the skills discussed in the explanation. Involve as many of the audience's senses as possible.

- **Application.** Application is the participants' chance to perform, to begin to develop their selling skills. A large amount of time should be devoted to this stage. Role plays, assignments, task groups and field exercises all can be used.

- **Examination/Evaluation.** By examination and evaluation you can determine the extent to which your objectives have been met. This can be accomplished during training by using questions, role plays, etc., or at the end of training by using written examinations. Examinations should be used only to serve a definite purpose and to help the participants remember key points.

- **Summary.** Here is where you bring everything together. Key points should be repeated and a strong closing statement should be used extolling the benefits of the material to the group. Participants should leave the session with a high degree of enthusiasm.

Training Hints

The final areas to cover are how to be as effective as possible in your delivery and how to control nervousness.

Enhancing Delivery

- Look and talk to your audience. Establish and maintain eye contact. Use participants' names whenever possible.
- Be and look alert.
- Pay attention to the volume of your voice (be loud enough to be heard by everyone without being too loud), your rate of delivery, enunciation, expressions (both verbal and non-verbal), tone and pitch (both should be varied).

Controlling nervousness

- Be thoroughly prepared.
- Project a good self-image; present yourself as a success.

- Carefully prepare your opening comments. You may want to begin by summarizing a previous session (yours or someone else's) that relates to the current session or telling a short story that introduces the material.
- Recognize and believe in the value of the material you will be covering.
- Watch for physical distractions, including your own appearance. For instance, if you exhibit a lack of interest to the participants, a roomful of disinterested participants is what you'll get.
- Watch for repeated use of mannerisms, such as leaning on the podium, placing hands in pockets, and playing with a pointer or pen. Also be wary of overused words or phrases.
- Use notes without reading them.

The two best hints, however, are to watch and learn from others and to examine yourself and the reaction you get from your audience.

There is no question that much needs to be covered and remembered before you are ready to present an effective training program. Before we discuss sales meetings and other types of ongoing training sessions, a brief look at how you can measure the success of a training program will complete our coverage of the steps to developing such a program.

9 Evaluating Results and Reinforcing Training

When you evaluate the results of your training program, you are determining whether you have met your training objectives. How you make this determination depends largely on what your objectives are.

If one of your objectives is to teach the proper technique for "listing sources of buyers," there are several ways that you can evaluate your training program participants' ability to fulfill the objective. One way would be to ask a general question and take answers from the group. If the group is not very large, you will be able to determine if each individual can provide at least one answer. With larger groups, you only will receive answers from a few individuals, so you will not be able to evaluate everyone's ability to list sources.

To fully evaluate the participants, you must deal with them in one-on-one situations using verbal questioning. During review and counseling sessions, the sales manager can discuss with the individual associates how they plan to find and work with buyers. These review and counseling sessions are a good way to check on what the associates learned in the training sessions, plus they provide an opportunity to evaluate or create action plans with the associates. Though time-consuming, this probably is the best way to evaluate and reinforce knowledge and attitude.

Another evaluation method is to use written examinations. These are effective in judging how well participants have memorized certain information. By using examinations, the trainer and associates (and the sales manager if the results are shared) can determine whether the material has been understood and retained. Examinations, however, take time to create and score. You may want to use them for only part of your training program. Another drawback is that many people tend to worry about taking tests. As a result they focus their attention on trying to hear what the right answer will be to questions they think will be asked. This may cause participants to miss much of what is being covered.

If another of your objectives is for the participants to be able to demonstrate dialogue to use with each of the major sources of listings to obtain a listing presentation appointment, you probably would want to use a role play to judge the participants' ability to meet the objectives. You could observe participants interacting in small groups and listen to parts of each demonstration, or you could have the individual associates role play with you. Because of the limited exposure the participants have had to this skill and the brief time they have had to practice it, you should not expect their performance to be perfect. Instead, you should look for basic abilities that can be further developed later.

Attitude is the third area that must be examined. You do this by observing the participants. How are the individual participants reacting to training and to the idea of performing the various selling activities that are being covered? While this is not an easy determination to make, it is important to do so and to candidly share your findings with participants on a one-on-one basis. A real estate sales associate's attitude affects his or her use of the knowledge that was acquired and the skills that were developed in the training program. And it definitely affects their listing and selling success!

Evaluations can be conducted during or at the end of each training session or at the end of the entire training program. But what about after the training program has concluded? As indicated previously, if a person has not acquired certain knowledge or cannot perform a certain skill, this is a training problem. By going through training, participants should at least learn fundamental skills and be able to perform them. If the associates do not apply the knowledge and skills in the field, this is a sales management problem.

To derive real benefits from training, there must be constant observation and reinforcement from management in the field. For example, to cover a subject during training such as developing a listing farm and then to not reinforce this training in the field is a waste of everyone's time. This normally does not happen if the sales manager is also the trainer. If someone else handles the training, the associates' manager must know what material is being covered and must make plans to help the associates use it. If this is not the case, then the training should be modified to more accurately reflect what will be performed in the field.

Don't forget, if something is worth doing, it is worth measuring. Through observation and various types of evaluation and examination you can fairly accurately determine the effectiveness of your training.

10

Ongoing Training

Ongoing training should be designed to meet the specific needs of the company, office, individual associates or groups of associates. Some training sessions, such as those covering a new marketing program or a new financing program, are appropriate for everyone. Other sessions will be useful for only a few or even one of your associates. The responsibility of making this determination lies with the sales manager. The manager must constantly look for areas that will help the associates improve their production. While some associates are self-starters and will attend programs on their own, most need to receive encouragement.

External programs can include the following:

- Board of REALTOR® seminars
- Real estate schools
- Courses conducted by the various institutes, societies and councils of the NATIONAL ASSOCIATION OF REALTORS®
- Lending institution programs
- University, college and community college courses either for academic credits or licensing credits, and extension programs for credits or certification
- National and state REALTOR® association conventions
- Commercially promoted programs by national speakers presented on a local basis

In-house training programs can be conducted by company personnel or outside experts, normally address specific needs, and can take the form of special sessions or sales meetings. Special sessions usually are conducted to fulfill a specific need. Sales meetings are best used to provide opportunities for the sales manager to present short training segments on certain areas in which the sales associates need help and encouragement. Because sales meetings tend to cover a wide range of

information, such as updates on listings, financing and new procedures, many managers conduct two meetings a week—one for updat-
ing and sharing information and the second for training. The second
meeting might be held each week or every other week, depending on
office needs.

Following is a list of reasons to hold sales meetings. These reasons
also can serve as the general objectives of the meetings.

- Sales meetings provide a structured opportunity for two-way communication between associates and management.
- They offer an opportunity to introduce new or revised policies and
  procedures and to review ones already in existence.
- They provide a chance to share new information with everyone at
  the same time, such as new laws or regulations, changes in mortgage
  lending, market updates, and updates on office listings and sales activity.
- They provide a time for recognizing accomplishments, boosting mo-
  rale and generating team spirit.
- They offer an opportunity to educate, train and problem solve.

The guidelines for establishing the proper environment for your
sales meetings are the same as those for training. Sales meetings
should be held at the same time and place each week unless a special
event is taking place. Unlike the more structured training format, sales
meetings should be very flexible so that side issues and problems can
be handled. Also, during a typical non-training sales meeting the manager should act as a moderator, leader and lecturer, thus providing for
the greatest amount of two-way communication. Finally, sales meetings should not just end, they should conclude on a high note. This
usually is the only time the manager has everyone together, so it is a
great opportunity to get everyone feeling good about themselves, the
office and company, and the real estate business.

Many managers find that attendance at sales meetings becomes a
problem. This can be overcome if associates feel that the meetings are
worthwhile and that they will learn something to help them make more
money. Also, if each associate is invited to participate, even if only to
share a bit of information about a listing, all of the associates will feel
more a part of what is going on. By developing team spirit, most associates will not want to miss meetings because they will feel that they are
not part of the team.

In addition, the manager should try to inject some fun into the
meetings. Fun does not have to dominate the meetings, but it can be
used to lighten the mood from time to time.

Keeping a sales meeting file of ideas and subjects will help you
prepare meetings that will be beneficial to your associates. The more
beneficial the meeting, the better attended it will be.

Finally, prepare and hand out an agenda or outline of topics to be
covered, including reports, announcements, activity updates and items
of mutual interest. A list of training objectives can be distributed if
part of the meeting will be focused on improving knowledge, skills and

attitude. Of course, you can also distribute the ever-popular commission and referral checks as well.

Ongoing training also is used to deal with specific needs, such as changes in the market or in buyer/seller attitudes. Remember, if associates cannot do it, it is a training problem. If they will not do it, it is a sales-management problem.

If a company finds that its listing inventory has increased substantially and buyers are becoming more reluctant to make a decision to the point that average showings per sale have almost doubled, a special training session might be held on working with buyers. At the same time new or revised materials and tools can be introduced.

The "Instructor's Outline" that follows is an example of a training session designed to take about three hours. The session was created because both the company and sales associates needed to increase sales. A review-type approach to the session was taken, as all of the associates had been through formal training and all had varying degrees of time in the business and success. The emphasis of the training was on the qualification process. As part of the session, a new buyer qualification form was introduced. The session also was used to kick off a company-wide sales contest. The outline that follows was for the sales manager to use. An outline created for the associates was the same, except that the notes and comments were excluded.

Instructor's Outline

OBJECTIVES: As a result of this training session, the participants will be able to:

- Discuss sources and methods of finding potential buyers
- Describe how to obtain buyer qualification appointments
- List the areas to be covered during the buyer qualification appointment
- Explain how to use the buyer analysis form
- Describe the rest of the process of working with buyers, including showing properties, obtaining an offer, writing the purchase agreement, the closing, the move-in, and following up

I. GENERATING BUYERS

    A. Pro-active, or active prospecting: The sales associate initiates the contact. (Note: *Be sure to cover how it will be done, when to call, what to say. Discuss the following.*)

     1. Sphere of influence
     2. Farming
     3. Warm canvassing
     4. For Sale By Owners—buyer and/or referral
     5. Expired listings—buyer and/or referral
     6. Others? (Note: *Ask the group. They should be able to come up with a few other sources. Be prepared to write them down.*)

B. Reactive, or passive prospecting: The buyer initiates the contact; the associate waits for the telephone to ring. (Note: *This is the least desirable from a management point of view. Still, your associates must be good at converting suspects into prospects. Discuss the how-to's for each of the following.*)

     1. Converting ad/sign calls (Note: *Stress the importance of being prepared.*)

       a. Answering the telephone
       b. Establishing rapport
       c. Gaining control
       d. Asking questions
       e. Obtaining buyer qualification appointment

     Instructor notes:

     Cover each of these points. Rather than lecturing, ask associates how each of these steps should be performed. Be prepared to expand on each one.

     Remember, the objective in answering an ad or sign call is to get a buyer qualification appointment.

     Set up a brief role play so participants can practice what has been discussed.

     2. Open houses (Note: *While sending out announcements and holding open houses initially are pro-active activities, they become passive once the door is unlocked. The key is to convert the open-house visitor into a prospect by obtaining a buyer qualification appointment. Some associates say they can do this at the open house. While some qualification can be accomplished this way, good in-depth qualification is difficult because of the lack of privacy. Discuss the following.*)

       a. Announcing the open house
       b. Determining activities to maximize the effectiveness of the open house
       c. Using marketing tools
       d. Greeting visitors
       e. Showing visitors the home
       f. Converting visitors to buyer qualification appointments
       g. Following up with visitors

II. CONDUCTING BUYER QUALIFICATION APPOINTMENTS

A. Where to conduct the appointment (Note: *Most experts agree that the buyers' home is the best place. The sales associate can see how they live, which many times is not the same as what comes across in conversation. Also, the buyers are more at ease and will be likely to more fully reveal their wants, needs, motivations and financial ability. If it is not possible to meet in the buyers' home, the second best place is in your office.*)

B. What to take on the appointment

1. Buyer needs analysis form
2. Sample purchase and sales agreements
3. Company brochures
4. Other materials? (Note: *Have the participants list the materials they would take, such as calculator, rate sheets, referral form, etc.*)

C. How to conduct the appointment

1. Setting up where to sit
2. Establishing rapport and control
3. Letting the buyers know you will be asking pertinent personal questions to determine their needs, wants, motivations and financial ability (Note: *It is very important that associates tell buyers that they will be asking questions and what the benefit of this is to the buyers. Ask the associates how they would do this and be prepared to provide your own examples.*)
4. Following a sequence (Note: *Divide the associates into small groups of four or five and ask them to complete the "Buyer Qualification Appointment Sequence Exercise." Reproduce the following page to hand out.*)
5. Using the buyer needs analysis form (Note: *Discuss when and how to use this form. Key aspects should include the following.*)

   a. Introductory techniques. Example: "Mr. and Mrs. Buyer, in order for me to help you find the home you desire, I need to ask you a few questions about what you are looking for. Would it be okay if I take a few notes while I ask you some questions?" (Note: *A yes answer is one small commitment from the buyers to work with the associate. You should be prepared to give one or two more.*)

   b. Quick qualifiers (Note: *The quick qualifier was a form used to establish an initial price range for a buyer. Many people feel that this is a sensitive area. An associate should begin by using the feature/benefit*

Buyer Qualification
Appointment Sequence Exercise

(handout)

OBJECTIVES: As a result of this exercise, the participants
will be able to:

- List the major areas/points to cover in a buyer
  qualification appointment.

- Describe the order to follow.

INSTRUCTIONS:

- Select a group leader.

- Choose a reporter.

- List all the major areas/points that you feel should be
  covered in a buyer qualification appointment. Arrange
  your list in the order you believe works best.

- You will have _____ minutes to complete this exercise.

- Be prepared to make a _____ minute report.

approach.) Example: "Mr. and Mrs. Buyer, I now have a feeling for what you are looking for in a home. Next I would like to establish a price range. To do this, I will need to ask you some questions about financing your new home. The benefit to you is that this will help us target the price range that would be most comfortable for you. Also, it will let me know if there is any special documentation that a lender will require. First..."

6. Discussing how to make an offer and the process that is followed from purchase agreement through closing

7. Obtaining a commitment (Note: *This is a critical step to selling success. The sales associate must obtain the buyers' verbal commitment that they will work with him or her. Stress that to obtain buyer loyalty, the associate must earn it and ask for it! Cover how associates can earn and ask for this commitment.*)

III. SELECTING PROPERTIES TO SHOW

A. What properties to select, based on the buyer qualification appointment

1. Types of properties
2. Styles of homes
3. Price range
4. Possible advisability of showing the buyers homes that do not quite meet their description

B. How many properties to select for each showing session

IV. SHOWING PROPERTIES

A. How to get there (do extra value selling along the way—neighborhood, general area, conveniences)

B. Information to provide in advance (avoid overkill and personal opinions)

C. How to approach the home

D. What to do and say if the sellers are at home

E. How to take the buyers through the home (Note: *Ask the associates for their opinions and experiences.*)

F. "Take the buyers' temperature."

1. Trial closes (Note: *Be prepared with a few examples.*)
2. Watch for buying signals (Note: *Have associates help you list some buying signals.*)
3. Based on the buyers' response you can:

a. Move on
b. Spend more time

c. Move on and return (Note: *Ask the participants for suggestions and be prepared with your own.*)

G. What to do if the buyers do not make an offer the first time out (Note: *Stay in frequent touch and try to set up a second appointment. As long as the buyers have the need, desire, financial ability and motivation, do not lose them to someone else. Remember that now it takes more showings per buyer to make a sale. Also, you may need to further qualify the buyers. The key is consistent two-way communication.*)

V. WRITING THE PURCHASE AGREEMENT

A. Key aspects of negotiation to remember

1. Price
2. Terms
3. Possession
4. Personal property

B. What to include (Note: *Ask the associates what contingencies they think should be included.*)

1. Wording
2. Dates
3. Responsibilities
4. Other inclusions

C. What to exclude

VI. GETTING FROM PURCHASE AGREEMENT THROUGH CLOSING

A. Inspections (who goes and why?)

B. Removing financing contingencies (Note: *Cover the following areas and add others you feel are appropriate.*)

1. Buyers' responsibilities
2. Time frame
3. Documentation

C. Removing other contingencies

D. Keeping everyone informed

E. Preparing the buyer for the closing and attending the closing (Note: *Touch on these briefly as a reminder; emphasize key areas.*)

VII. AFTER THE MOVE-IN

A. Keeping in touch, even if it was a problem transaction (Note: *Recommend a personal follow-up program in addition to the one conducted by the company.*)

B. Asking for leads (Note: *Again, stress the importance of staying in touch.*)

VIII. SUMMARY (summarize key points)

Possible Topics for Continuous Training

Following is a list of possible topics for sales meetings and other forms of continuous training.

KNOWLEDGE TOPICS

- Too many listings—how to handle sellers and keep them happy
- Not enough listings—how to obtain more
- Writing effective ads
- Using a financial calculator
- Writing purchase agreements
- Taxation—changes in property and homeownership tax laws
- Methods of financing
- Setting goals
- Understanding what motivates sellers and buyers
- New financing programs

SKILLS TOPICS

- How to handle telephone inquiries from signs and newspaper advertising
- How to communicate during prospecting, qualifying, showing, negotiating and closing
- How and when to listen during prospecting, qualifying, showing, negotiating and closing
- Making warm canvassing calls
- Closing techniques
- Follow-up and servicing techniques
- Preparing and making listing presentations
- Servicing listings to sell—how to be creative
- FSBOs—how to approach and sell
- How to qualify buyers and gain their commitment to work with you
- How to work with unhappy buyers
- Personal time management

- Developing a farm
- Handling objections to reach a mutual understanding
- Negotiating price with buyers
- Negotiating price with sellers
- Understanding what motivates sellers and buyers

ATTITUDE TOPICS

- What a great business!
- Having fun while making sales
- Putting your self-image to work for you

OUTSIDE SPEAKERS

Outside speakers need basic information about who they will be talking to and why. Tell them the kinds of information and guidance they should supply (i.e., on knowledge, skills or attitude), the time limits for their presentation, and whether they will be asked questions. If they will be asked questions, make certain they agree to answer them. Confirm in writing when and where the meeting will be held. Following is a list of possible outside speakers.

- Chamber of commerce leaders
- Sales representatives—burglar alarm systems, pest inspectors, home inspectors, and any other business your people should know more about
- Home insurance brokers
- Telephone company representatives (how to use the phone professionally, etc.)
- Mortgage loan officers and originators
- Zoning commission members (new ordinances, etc.)
- Tax assessors (how properties are measured, how values are established, when and how to appeal assessments and taxes, etc.)
- Local officials (building codes, planning, public services, etc.)
- Appraisers (how they judge market value, what methods they use, etc.)
- Architects (building codes, planning, public services, zoning, building materials, renovating, converting, restoring old structures, etc.)
- Contractors/builders (construction techniques, costs, materials, etc.)
- Lawyers (legal situations encountered at closing, escrow, title variations, things to know about contracts, etc.)

- Accountants (accounting principles for personal records, how to keep good tax records, what buyers and sellers should know about homeownership taxation, etc.)

Summary

Training is the development of skills and attitude that enable people to put acquired knowledge to consistent and profitable use.

Within this definition is the implication that knowledge is already possessed by the participants or that it will be provided during the training. The word "consistent" indicates that effective training will cause people to develop behavior and habits necessary to accomplish their goals.

Reinforcement of the knowledge, skills and attitudes developed during training must be done as an ongoing function of management to maximize the impact of the training.

Training cannot stand alone. Training coupled with coaching and counseling will have a significant positive effect on a company's production level, market share and profitability if all are made a regular part of the company's management activity.

Appendix A: Sample Training Program

Following is a brief outline showing possible content and training methods for new sales associates. While reading through this material, consider the following:

1. Keep your program simple. Remember, these people are entering a new career, and although they have passed your state's licensing exam, it does not mean they know a lot about the sales business. They also do not need to be impressed by your extensive knowledge of the business. Focus on what they will need to know and do to get off to a productive and successful start.
2. Don't forget, the mind can absorb only as much as the behind can endure. Frequent breaks and activities that allow participants to at least stretch a bit can help overcome this potential problem.
3. Try to build in as much application as you can. If the participants don't apply the material they are being taught, they will forget it.
4. Remember, the learning methods in this book are suggestions. Be creative. When you take a course or attend a seminar, watch how the instructors present their material. This is an excellent way to sharpen your training skills and learn new training techniques.

Case studies and action plans have not been included in the outline. Case studies will depend on your area and company. Most of the assignment areas described in this outline are a form of case study where you provide the background and have the participants find a solution to the situation. Action plans can be used wherever you have an area that you want to follow up on and reinforce in the field.

The forms in Appendix B are included to help you develop your training program or sales meeting.

PROGRAM OBJECTIVE: As a result of this training program, the participants will be able to describe the process, functions and activities necessary to successfully list and sell residential real estate.

Session 1

OBJECTIVES: As a result of this session, the participants will be able to:

- Describe the objectives of the training program

- Briefly describe the company's history and organization

- Demonstrate a basic working knowledge of the company's market area and market conditions

- List major sources of listings

- Set up a sphere-of-influence list and contact system

■ *Subject I*

Training program objectives

Content

Your training program objectives will depend on your needs, your company structure and procedures, market conditions, and possibly the competition.

Presentation Methods

Town Hall. Before you give the program objectives, ask the participants what they would like to know and be able to do as a result of the program.

You might start by having the participants write down their expectations. Next, form them into small groups. Have the participants within these groups share some expectations with the rest of their group, and have the group choose several representative expectations it agrees upon. Have all the participants come together again and have each group share its first two expectations. After everyone has finished, ask if there are any burning issues left. The list you have written down on the flip chart or transparency indicates the participants' objectives. You should make a commitment to accomplish theirs as well as yours. From time to time during the program you can refer back to the list and ask if the participants think their objectives are being accomplished.

■ Subject II

Company history and organization

Content

History of the company from beginning to present, major events, honors, recognition of the company and individuals; company structure and organization

Presentation Methods

Lecture. Encourage the participants to ask questions.

Materials: Hand out company brochures, organizational charts, job descriptions, the written history of the company, biographical sketches of key individuals, etc.

■ Subject III

Market area and conditions

Content

Map showing primary and secondary markets; MLS and governmental data describing the markets, price ranges, selling time, etc.; nature of the competition, community, property taxation, and characteristics of schools, etc.; special laws on consumerism, misrepresentation, etc.

Presentation Methods

Participative lecture. Rather than just tell the participants, ask them for their impressions of market conditions and the market in general. Be prepared to fill in areas they miss.

Materials: Hand out MLS information, governmental data, etc. Try to keep it simple.

■ Subject IV

Sources of listings

Content

Importance of listings; overview of the listing process; prospecting as the key to listing and sales success

Presentation Methods

Lecture. Develop a flow chart of the listing process to help the participants follow along.

Ask the participants to name major listing sources. Be prepared to move their answers into what you feel are major categories, such as FSBOs, expired listings, spheres of influence, farming and warm canvassing. Spend time on each of the major sources of listings.

■ Subject V

Set up a sphere-of-influence list and contact system.

Content

How a sphere-of-influence list and contact system generates leads that can turn into listings and sales

Presentation Methods

Lecture. Explain the importance of using a sphere of influence and show how to set one up.

Materials: Show the participants your personal sphere-of-influence system as an example. Provide supplies and materials for them to set up their own systems. Do not skip this part. If you ask them to go out and find their own supplies, it will take forever.

Assignment: Give the participants a set period of time to create their systems and bring them in to show you. The purpose of the assignment is to immediately get the participants involved in an activity that will help them in their listing and selling efforts. Further coverage of prospecting for listings is outlined in Session 4.

Session 2

OBJECTIVES: As a result of this session, the participants will be able to:

• Describe effective communication techniques

• Demonstrate how to correctly answer the telephone and handle "ad" calls

■ Subject I

Communication

Content

Establishing rapport; two-way versus one-way communication; questioning techniques; telephone and face-to-face communication; answering the telephone, gaining control, obtaining appointments

(Note: The placement of this section will depend on your company's policy on when an individual has earned the opportunity to start answering the phone. If you move this session, you may want to also consider moving Session 3.)

Presentation Methods

Lecture/demonstration. Describe in detail how to use effective two-way communication in person and on the telephone. Demonstrate the correct methods.

Task group. Have the participants discuss methods that they feel would be effective with different types of people.

Role play. Have someone with basic buyer information "call in" to a sales associate. The associate's job is to get an appointment without giving out too much information. If possible, use real telephones in two different rooms and, if possible, put a speaker phone on the receiving end so that everyone will be able to listen to the conversation.

Session 3

OBJECTIVE: As a result of this session, the participants will be able to:

- Demonstrate questioning, closing, objection handling and negotiating techniques

■ Subject I

Communication

Content

Mastering the techniques of questioning, closing, handling objections and negotiating

Presentation Methods

Lecture/demonstration. Describe the techniques and give at least one example of each. Use someone in the group to demonstrate the techniques.

Role play. Techniques for closing and handling objections should be built into role-playing exercises in other parts of your training. If you have already covered listings, for example, then give the participants a situation involving a seller who is having trouble reaching a decision about signing the listing agreement. Provide enough detail so the participants have points to work from, then set up groups and rotate the roles.

If you have not covered subject areas that lend themselves to good role-playing exercises on closing, then develop a simple situation. Even though the participants will not have enough knowledge or skill to do an outstanding job of closing, handling objections, etc., the experience will provide them with a beginning understanding of the importance of the techniques.

Materials: Hand out sample dialogue for closing and handling objections.

(Note: The techniques taught here should be basic. This subject area is a good one to come back to at a later time, perhaps during sales meetings.)

Session 4

OBJECTIVES: As a result of this session, the participants will be able to:

- Demonstrate how to prospect the major sources of listings

- Demonstrate dialogue to use with each of the major sources to obtain a listing-presentation appointment

- List the steps necessary to prepare for a listing-presentation appointment

■ Subject I

Prospecting for listings

Content

Spheres of influence, farming, FSBOs, expireds, warm canvassing

Presentation Methods

Lecture. Ask the participants to name major sources. Give brief explanations of approaches for each.

Task group. Break into groups by source. Have the participants discuss methods of prospecting, sales tools they might use, and possible dialogue to use in obtaining a listing-presentation appointment. They will not know all the answers. In fact, they may come up with only a couple of ideas. What they come up with will provide you with a base on which to build.

Materials: Have samples of company marketing materials available.

■ Subject II

Prospecting dialogue

Content

Sample dialogue to use with each source

Presentation Methods

Demonstration. If possible, have the participants demonstrate their dialogue from the task-group exercise. You should also demonstrate an approach, use of materials and dialogue for each major source.

Materials: Hand out sample dialogue for each source.

Role play. Have the participants use their approaches and yours in a role-play exercise that involves calling on a listing prospect, and if appropriate, attempting to obtain a listing appointment.

■ Subject III

Listing-appointment preparation

Content

Steps necessary to be prepared to make a listing presentation, which will depend on your company policies and procedures, MLS policies and procedures, and local market conditions

Presentation Methods

Lecture. List the steps and describe where and how the material is to be obtained and used. Demonstrate completion of forms.

Materials: Hand out both blank and completed forms.

Assignment: Have the participants prepare a market analysis listing and presentation packets on their own homes. Give them a completion date. (See Session 5.)

Session 5

OBJECTIVES: As a result of this session, the participants will be able to:

- Demonstrate the completion of the preparation steps necessary to make a listing presentation

- Describe the key elements in making a listing presentation

- Explain the content of the company's listing-presentation book or materials

- Discuss how to make a presentation and close for an appointment

- List the major steps in developing a marketing plan to sell the property

■ Subject I

Listing-appointment preparation

Content

Discussion of the participants' completed assignment from the previous session

Presentation Methods

Application. Discuss what the participants experienced when they attempted to complete this assignment. Answer all of their questions and fill in the gaps in their knowledge. You may want to have them turn in their assignments so you can make suggestions privately on an individual basis.

■ Subject II

Making a listing presentation

Content

Key elements to a listing presentation, use of a listing-presentation book or presentation materials, making a presentation, and closing for the listing

Presentation Methods

Lecture. Discuss major segments and elements of a listing presentation, including closing for the listing.
   Task group. Have the participants break into small task groups and develop ideas that could be used during an appointment. Depending on the overall group size, you may want to assign each task group a major segment to work on.

■ Subject III

Listing-presentation book or materials

Content

Explanation on the content of the book, why the material is there, how to use it

Presentation Methods

Demonstration. Demonstrate the use of the listing-presentation book or materials by using the key segments and elements as stepping stones to obtaining the listing.
   Task group. Have the participants form task groups and discuss ways to personalize the book or materials. Have each group report its suggestions.

Application. Have the participants personalize their copies of
the book or materials as an assignment and be prepared to use
them at a later session in a role-play exercise.

(Note: If your company does not have a prepared listing
presentation book, you can change this section to have the
participants develop their own.)

■ Subject IV

Closing for the listing

Content

Using key elements of the presentation—such as information about
the company, a marketing plan, a discussion of listing price,
etc.—to reach commitment

Presentation Methods

Participative lecture/demonstration. Tie into preparation and
presentation steps. Ask the participants for their suggestions and
what they would do to close. Then demonstrate how to close and
obtain the listing.

Role play. A role-play exercise on the listing presentation is
coming up in Session 6, Subject 1.

Lecture. Explain how to complete a listing agreement/contract.

■ Subject V

Marketing plan

Content

Development of a marketing plan, including the major steps in
marketing a property and the materials to use

Presentation Methods

Lecture. Discuss your company's procedure for marketing listings
and the methods and tools available to successfully market listings.
Ask the participants for their suggestions.

Demonstration. Show how to develop a marketing plan with the
sellers' input.

Assignment. Have the participants practice a listing presentation
using the data they put together from the previous assignment in

Session 4, Subject III, their listing-presentation books and other company materials. Tell them they will be role playing this during a future session (tell them which one). You also may want to have them complete a listing agreement. In addition, have them develop a marketing plan for the property.

Materials: Have available a listing presentation book, listing agreements, marketing tools, and a sample marketing plan.

Session 6

OBJECTIVES: As a result of this session, the participants will be able to:

- Demonstrate how to make a listing presentation and how to ask for the listing

- Explain the elements of a marketing plan for a specific property

■ Subject I

Listing presentation

Content

The participants' materials and a demonstration of a listing presentation

Presentation Methods

Role play. Have the participants demonstrate how to make a listing presentation using the materials they have prepared, their listing presentation books or materials, their completed market analysis, company marketing tools, and their marketing plan (assuming they reach agreement on the listing).

■ Subject II

Marketing plan

Content

Participants' sample marketing plan

Presentation Methods

Discussion. Have the participants share their plans and ideas on how to market their listings.

■ Subject III

The listing process

Content

Key elements in obtaining marketable listings

Presentation Methods

Lecture. Summarize the listing process. Refer to your flow chart.

Session 7

OBJECTIVES: As a result of this session, the participants will be able to:

- Describe the process of working with buyers
- List sources of potential buyers
- Demonstrate dialogue to use when first contacting prospective buyers
- Describe the major areas to cover when qualifying buyers

■ Subject I

Selling process

Content

Major areas of working with buyers, including prospecting, qualifying, selecting and showing homes, writing the purchase agreement and negotiating the offer

Presentation Methods

Lecture. Develop a flow chart to show the process of working with buyers.

■ Subject II

Prospecting for buyers

Content

Major sources of buyers; dialogue to use when contacting potential buyers

Presentation Methods

Town hall. Ask the participants to name the most productive sources for buyers. Be prepared to fill in anything they might miss, such as spheres of influence, warm canvassing, farming, and conducting open houses.

Task group. Break the participants into small task groups and assign one or two sources to each. Have them share the dialogue they develop with the entire group. Be prepared to comment on the positive aspects of their reports and build upon the bases they establish.

Materials: Provide any buyer-prospecting tools that you have.

Role play. Break into groups of three and have the participants role play using the dialogue and prospecting tools that have been developed during the session.

■ Subject III

Buyer qualification

Content

Major areas to cover in qualifying buyers, such as their needs, wants, financial ability, motivation, time frame and knowledge of the buying process

Presentation Methods

Lecture/demonstration. Discuss how to set up the appointment, how to open, what areas to cover, how to ask personal questions, and what to do to obtain the buyer's verbal commitment. Cover any forms you have to help qualify buyers. Show how to ask questions to draw out the responses of buyers.

Assignment: Have the participants review their information on buyer qualification and be prepared to role play an appointment at the next session.

Materials: Provide buyer qualification forms.

 # Session 8

OBJECTIVES: As a result of this session, the participants will be able to:

- Demonstrate a buyer qualification appointment

- Explain how to select properties to show

- Describe how to demonstrate properties

■ Subject I

Buyer qualification

Content

Conducting a buyer qualification appointment

Presentation Methods

Lecture. Briefly review the process, then ask for questions.

Role play. Break into groups of three and provide the "buyers" with data sheets about their needs, desires, finances, etc. At the conclusion of the role playing, summarize the key aspects of a qualification appointment. You also may want to demonstrate certain areas.

■ Subject II

Property selection

Content

How to select properties to show to a prospective buyer based on the information learned during the qualification appointment

Presentation Methods

Lecture. The specific content will depend on your MLS and local regulations. Emphasize that selection is based on what is learned during the qualification process.

■ Subject III

Showing property

Content

How to demonstrate a property to help the buyer make a decision to buy

Presentation Methods

Lecture. Discuss what information to give the buyer, what to do and say in transit, how to show the property, how to ask questions, when and how to close, how to handle objections.

Assignment: Have the participants practice showing their own home or a vacant office listing to someone. Tell them you will be setting up appointments to have them show you through actual listings. Or you may want to have their manager be involved with the practice showings.

(Note: It's great if you can arrange field trips with a couple of associates at a time so they can role play showing actual homes.)

Session 9

OBJECTIVES: As a result of this session, the participants will be able to:

- Demonstrate the completion of a purchase agreement

- Describe the negotiation process and the key elements in negotiation

- Demonstrate how to present a purchase agreement to the sellers

■ Subject I

The purchase agreement

Content

How to complete a purchase agreement

Presentation Methods

Lecture. Explain how to complete a purchase agreement using a filled-in handout example.

Individual activity: Give the participants the necessary details and have them complete a purchase agreement during this session. If there is not enough time to do this, make it an assignment to be completed and discussed at the next session. Either way, be sure to discuss what they did and to answer any questions they might have.

■ Subject II

Negotiation

Content

The negotiation process and the key elements of negotiation, such as price, terms, possession and personal property

Presentation Methods

Lecture/demonstration. Describe how to prepare and present purchase agreements to sellers. Briefly discuss how to reach an agreement between the parties. You should set up a brief demonstration of this step.

(Note: There is a separate session on closing, handling objections and negotiation.)

Role play. Break into groups. Give the people playing the sellers information about what they want from the sale—price, terms, possession date, personal property, etc. Give those playing the sales associates the basic information they need. Be sure to rotate the sales associate role so everyone has a chance. You should develop several different situations and sets of information so the participants do not get bored when you rotate roles.

(Note: The participants will experience some frustration because of their lack of knowledge about and skills at closing, handling objections and negotiating, unless you have covered these areas in earlier sessions. A little frustration is OK; it can help encourage the participants to want to learn how to handle these situations.)

■ Subject III

The selling process

Content

Summary

Presentation Methods

Wrap-up the role play and summarize the selling process.

Sessions 10 and 11

OBJECTIVES: As a result of these sessions, the participants will be able to:

- Describe the use of three forms of mortgage financing

- Demonstrate how to determine a buyer's mortgage amount, purchase price, monthly investment and estimated closing costs

■ Subject I

Types of mortgage financing

Content

Will depend on your market

Presentation Methods

Lecture. Keep it simple. They will probably forget much of what you cover. Plan on doing a follow-up session.

■ Subject II

Financial qualification

Content

Financial qualification to determine purchase price, mortgage amount, monthly investment, and estimated closing costs

Presentation Methods

Lecture/demonstration. This will depend on your market and current economic conditions. You also should help the participants learn to use a financial calculator by showing its correct operation during the session. It helps if each participant has a calculator to work with while you are covering this area.

Individual activity: Give the participants buyer information and have them perform the calculations.

(Note: Timing will depend on the types of financing discussed and how much in-depth coverage you give to using the financial calculator. This is why two sessions are suggested for this subject area.)

Session 12

OBJECTIVES: As a result of this session, the participants will be able to:

- Describe at least two methods to organize their time

- Demonstrate how to set business goals

■ Subject I

Time management

Content

Importance of time management, ways to prioritize and schedule time, ways to balance business and personal time

Presentation Methods

Lecture. Describe and discuss time management. You should consider buying or renting one or more of the many excellent videos or films that are available on time management. Use the video or film as the basis for your discussion. Provide everyone with a sample pocket calendar or a schedule sheet as an example of the type of format that works.

Individual activity: Have the participants fill out schedules for themselves that include everything they think they should do during a typical week.

Task group. Break the participants into groups and have them come up with a week's schedule they would recommend.

Assignment: Have the participants develop a schedule of activities for the next month. Indicate that you or their manager will be setting up appointments with each of them to review their schedules along with their goals, which is the next subject area.

Materials: Some type of scheduling sheets or appointment books should be used.

■ Subject II

Setting goals

Content

Will depend on your philosophy

Presentation Methods

Lecture. Emphasize the importance of setting goals and describe how to do it using your regular worksheets and forms.

Assignment: Have them set preliminary goals, and tell them that you or their manager will be making appointments to review their goals along with their time-management schedules.

Materials: Provide goal-setting forms.

■ Subject III

Summary

Content

Review of the training program and what's ahead

Presentation Methods

Lecture. Give an overview of what you have covered and a short summary of what the participants can expect. Keep it positive!

Examination: You can use an examination prior to your summary. This is a more forced type of review, and will only gauge the participants' retention of the information presented. Still, it is an instructional stage worth considering.

Appendix B: Forms

The sample training program in Appendix A should provide you with a basic outline of what needs to be covered to get someone started on the path to a successful career in residential real estate sales. There are some areas you may want to expand on depending on your market, your company and you, but the sample can be used as the framework upon which to build your own program. The first two forms in this appendix can be completed for each session and used as handouts for the participants. The last form is a self-evaluation form for trainers.

SESSION TITLE _____

OBJECTIVES: As a result of this session, the participants will
            be able to:

SUBJECT:

CONTENT:

PRESENTATION METHODS:

Participant Evaluation

I learned the following during this training session:

The most important aspects to me were:

I plan to use the following (include how and when):

The benefits to me are:

Note: This form is designed to be a personal action plan and commitment sheet as opposed to just a hand-in evaluation of the training program. It is to be used at the end of training sessions and can be used at the end of the training program.

Trainer's Self-Evaluation

Trainer Characteristics	Did Very Well	Adequate	Need to Improve	Comments
Knowledge				
Communication				
People skills				
Self-image				
Confidence				
Enthusiasm				
Humor				
Voice				
Body language				
Methods Used	Did Very Well	Adequate	Need to Improve	Comments
Town hall				
Lecture				
Participative lecture				
Role play				
Task group				
Case study				
Action plan				
Coaching				
Involvement and feedback				

Trainer's Self-Evaluation (continued)

Audio/Visual Equipment Used	Did Very Well	Adequate	Need to Improve	Comments
Writing board				
Flip chart				
Handouts				
Overhead projector				
Transparencies				
Videotape				
Video camera				
Others:				

Index

A

Adults as learners 9–10
Attitude 2, 33–34, 60, 70–71
   see Three areas of training
Audio/visual aids 37–41, 50
   Audiocassette players/tapes 40
   Books 41
   Films 41
   Flipcharts 38
   Handout materials 38–39
   Overhead projectors 39
   Screens 39–40
   Slides 41
   Training Manuals 41
   Transparencies 41
   TVs 40
   VCRs/videotapes 40
   Writing boards 38

B

Behavior development 1–2
Benefits to company 4–7
   Control turnover 7
   Improve communications 7
   Improve company image 5–6
   Improve work habits 7
   Increase profits 4–5
   Recruiting 7
Benefits to sales associates 8
   Achieve higher earnings 8
   Increase self-confidence 8
   Recognize accomplishments 8
Budgeting 29–31
   Approaches 30
   Cost areas 31

C

Content (of training program)
   33–35
   Organizing 34–35
   Selecting 33–34
Customer orientation 5–6

D

Delivery 57
Doing process 1

E

Education 1
Evaluation 1–2, 52–53, 57,
   59–60, 95
   see Role play
   Questions and answers 59
   Review and counseling
     sessions 59
   Role play 60
   Written exams 59

F
First impressions 10
Five stages of training sessions
    56–57
    see Evaluation; presentation
        methods
    Application 57
    Evaluation/examination 57
    Preparation 56
    Presentation 56–57
    Summary 57
Four learning stages of training 3
    Conscious competent 3
    Conscious incompetent 3
    Unconscious competent 3
    Unconscious incompetent 3

I
Instructor's outline 63–68
Involvement/feedback 55–56
    see Presentation methods
    Directed questions 55
    Overhead questions 55
    Relayed questions 55–56
    Reversed questions 55

K
Knowledge 2–3, 33–34, 59–60,
    69, 71
    see Three areas of training

M
Marketing 5–6
    Place/delivery systems 6
    Pricing 6
    Products/services 6
    Promotion 6
Misconceptions (about training)
    8–9

N
Needs analysis 17–25
    Company/office 17–19
    Sales associate 19–24
Nervousness (how to control)
    57–58

O
Objectives 11–12, 25–27, 50
    see Strategic planning

General 25–26
Specific 26
Ongoing training 61–71
    External programs 61
    In-house 61–62
    Outside speakers 70–71
    Possible topics 69–70
    Sales meetings 61–63

P
"Participant" vs. "trainee"
    49–50
Presentation methods 49–56
    see Involvement/feedback;
        role play
    Action plan 54
    Case study 54
    Coaching 54–55
    Involvement/feedback 55–56
    Lecture 48–50
    Participative lecture 50
    Role play 50–53
    Task group 53–54
    Town hall 50

R
Reinforcement 1, 49 60
Role play 2, 50–53, 60
    see Presentation methods
    Multiple 51–53
    Spontaneous 51–52
    Structured 51–52
    Three basic steps 52–53

S
Sales management 2
Sales meetings 61–63
    see Ongoing training; training
        environment
    Attendance 62
    Environment 62
    Reasons to have 62
Sales training 62
Scheduling 48–49
    Full-day sessions 48–49
    Half-day sessions 49
    Weekend sessions 49
Seating arrangements 47–48
    see Training environment
    Chevron 47

Circle 47
Horseshoe 47–48
Roundtable 48
Self-starters 2
Skills 1–3, 33–35, 51, 59–60,
    69–71
    see Three areas of training
Strategic planning (SMOST
    approach) 11–13
    see Objectives
    Mission statement 11
    Objectives 11–12
    Situation analysis 11–12
    Strategies 12–13
    Tactics 12–13

T
Termination 7
Thinking process 1
Three areas of training 2, 33–35,
    59–60, 69–71
    see Attitude; knowledge; skills
Tracking 21–24
    Forms 23–24
Trainers 43–46
    Candidates 46
    Characteristics 43–45
Trainer's self-evaluation form 96
Training environment 46–48, 62
    see Seating arrangements
Training groups 2